Ireland's Wildlife Year

Ireland's Wildlife Year

General Editor Eric Dempsey

Contributors: Eric Dempsey, Declan Doogue, Tom Hayden

Photographers: Billy Clarke, Eric Dempsey, Carsten Krieger

Gill & Macmillan

Gill & Macmillan
Hume Avenue, Park West, Dublin 12
with associated companies throughout the world
www.gillmacmillan.ie

© Text: Eric Dempsey, Declan Doogue, Tom Hayden 2011
© Photographs: Billy Clarke, Eric Dempsey, Carsten Krieger 2011
978 07171 5007 6

All mammal photographs by Billy Clarke, unless otherwise noted.
All bird photographs by Eric Dempsey.
All flora/landscape photographs by Carsten Krieger.

Design and print origination by illuminate creative consultancy
Printed and bound in Italy by Printer Trento SpA

This book is typeset in Garamond 11 on 15pt.

The paper used in this book comes from the wood pulp of managed forests.
For every tree felled, at least one tree is planted, thereby renewing natural resources.

A CIP catalogue record for this book is available from the British Library.

1 3 5 4 2

Contents

Acknowledgments

As always, there are many people who have given great encouragement, advice and support in so many ways that it really is impossible to include all their names here.

However, special mention must be given to Michael O'Clery, Fergus Fitzgerald, John Fox, Philip Clancy and Gerald Franck for their honest feedback and suggestions during the early drafts of this book.

For their combination of support, suggestions and advice, I would also like to thank Sarah Carty, Richard Collins, Shay Connolly, Anna Digby, Eddie Dunne, Terry Flanagan, Hazel Johnston, Andrea Kelly, Paul Kelly, Anthony McGeehan, Siobhan McNamara, Derek Mooney, Éanna ní Lamhna and Helen Quinn.

Eric Dempsey
General Editor

An Introduction to the Seasons

Even within our temperature-controlled and over-illuminated homes and workplaces there can hardly be one among us who is not aware of the passage of the seasons. How much more keenly are these changes felt by our flora and fauna that must cope with the regular cycles of cold, wet, heat and drought! There are hard times to be endured and survived, and there are times of plenty when the living is easier. These seasonal changes are the backdrop to the two great dramas in which every living organism must play its part ... the struggle to survive and the imperative to reproduce.

Positioned on the western fringe of Europe, Ireland is greatly influenced by the sea, warmed by the waters of the Gulf Stream and by the rain-laden winds coming off the Atlantic, especially to the western sides of the island. The contrast between the winter and summer temperatures is far less extreme than it is in central Europe. Within Ireland the climate of the sunny south-east is very different from that of the western seaboard, not only as measured crudely in terms of total annual rainfall, but in the number of days on which the rain falls and the sun shines.

PLANTS

For plants, the combined influences of climate, weather and seasonality exert a profound effect on the distribution and the order of appearance of individual species through the year. Cumulatively, and in complex interactions with local environmental conditions, they also influence the types of semi-natural vegetation that develop in different locations. The Irish 'soft day' is highly significant for species such as mosses and liverworts, plants that require a more or less continuously damp atmosphere. Conversely many species from the south and east of Europe require intense spells of bright and hot weather to bring them to the point where they can flower and set seed successfully. Within these broad climatic determinants there are many apparent and contrasting exceptions. Arid hot spots on shallow soils formed over bare rock, sunny south-facing roadside banks, north-facing ravines, damp shady caves, all exert powerful constraints on species-occurrence at local level. But survive they do, each individual species equipped with its individual environmental strengths and ecological frailties. Collectively they respond to the changes that take place as the earth takes its annual ellipsoidal tour around the sun, its axis tilting one way and then the other, resulting in what we call the seasons.

Our perceptions of seasonality are driven largely by our own restricted contacts with it, perceptions conditioned by our largely urbanised existences. Alterations in day length, temperature, sunlight, freezing and warming all have their influences, but many of the changes are not immediately evident to house dwellers. The first stirrings of native plants are usually most obvious early in the year. Plants with buds formed just below ground level start first, not needing to germinate from seed. They, and the plants developing from seed, must grow fast in the race for light. By high summer most deciduous woods are thrust into a cooler and shaded state, as the tree canopy closes, cutting off light to the woodland floor. Nearer to home, the lawn needs to be cut and then cut more often. Weeds grow faster. Dandelions create great swathes of yellow, their flowering stems growing at more than a centimetre a day, until their parachute seeds, released in their millions, proclaim the end of spring.

By early summer the soil has been gradually warming up. Pools, formed during winter flooding, begin to dry out as the water table falls. After a winter in slatted sheds and a diet of preserved food stored from the previous year as silage and hay, cattle are released into pastures to feed on the fresh plant life that has re-sprouted during their confinement. Days are longer and the surge of growth continues. Reduced rainfall diminishes the supply of water to streams and rivers, lowering the levels of the lakes into which they flow. Bare, muddy areas are exposed, allowing an array of fast-growing, short-lived plants to flourish on open, nutrient-rich, warm mud. Taller, emergent species on the shoreline, with inflorescences formed well above the surface of the shallow warm waters, open their flowers. True aquatics can rise and fall, tracking fluctuating water levels, their submerged or buoyant vegetative parts being robust enough to support their short-lived flowering stems.

The season of mists and mellow fruitfulness is aptly named. This is most evident in the network of hedgerows that cover most of our fertile lowlands. The flowers of bramble, rose, hawthorn and blackthorn form a natural harvest, producing blackberries, rose hips, haws and sloes. This abundance of edibles for birds, mammals and invertebrates, will in turn be converted into food reserves for hibernation and migration. The larger ferns, unrolling their fronds from spring, have by now produced and released their spores that waft about in the air until they come to earth and start the next generation.

As the days shorten the lawn grasses stop growing. The last cut is taken. Mosses of lawns and natural habitats come into their own. In the woodlands, leaves have been falling. Winter storms snap off weak branches, dislodge loose bark and fell ailing and poorly-rooted trees. The growth of the year is returned to the soil to be recycled by fungi, bacteria, insects, snails, slugs and other mainly soil-dwelling invertebrates, with lifestyles that are geared to thrive in the leaf-litter soil interface. In time, these layers deepen, dry on top but wet at the bottom. Many invertebrates, especially those that depend on living, growing leaves for food, have other strategies to get them through the winter when there is little in the way of active plant growth to provide new food. Some over-winter as eggs or pupae but others survive as larvae or even as adults. Leaf-litter dwellers can migrate downwards in the soil when the surface layers become too cold, just as they do in summer when the upper soil layers become too dry. Perennial plants close down most of their above-ground functions. Annuals, biennials and even perennials will have set and scattered seed, which then wait in cold storage until the following year.

As winter takes hold there is little new growth. Botanists at this time concentrate on mosses and liverworts which by now can be encountered in abundance, when their larger and faster growing flowering plant competitors die back. Slower growing plants such as lichens, intimately connected to and influenced by the substrates on which they grow, provide abundant material for investigation. Evidence of landscape history becomes more obvious as the covering of vegetation thins, hit by snows and frosts. The connections between the earth, the rocks and the plant cover become clearer, even on the shortest days when the sun rises late, sets early and seldom gets above the eye-line defined by the tallest trees. That clarity, so crisply evident, indicates the end and the new beginning, with all its individual nuances, fitting within a reassuringly consistent and recurrent time-frame.

MAMMALS

How the winter impacts on a mammal depends on a number of factors, chief of which is body size. Small mammals have a higher fuel consumption (i.e. energy requirement) for their size than do large mammals. Some small mammals, particularly those that feed on flying insects, opt out in winter and hibernate. So too does the Hedgehog. But hibernating is not just a matter of sleeping through bad times. It is a precisely regulated process that is beyond the capability of most species. For these, such as shrews, mice, voles, rats, Stoats, squirrels and larger mammals, they must continue as normal in so far as they can. Many compensate by having reduced appetites in winter, thus saving the energy that might fruitlessly be spent searching for food that may not be there. Some, such as squirrels and Woodmice, store food in times of plenty in secret caches that they hide for later use. Others, such as deer and Badgers, store resources in the form of body fat to be drawn down when times are hard or when energy is required faster than can be collected at the time.

Going hand in hand with survival is the problem of how and when to breed and produce as many offspring as possible. This raises the other major impact of a seasonal climate. There is a best time to be born and this timing may be crucial. As might be expected, survival of young is most likely when weather is warmer and food for the lactating mother or for the weaned young is abundant. Thus the females of almost all our mammals are usually involved in rearing young during late spring and high summer. However, while the best time to be born is commonly in the summer it does not follow that all our mammals mate at the same time of year. This is because larger species generally have larger offspring and these require a longer time to develop from an egg into a fetus that is ready to be born. This general dependence of the length of gestation on body size means that while there may be, in general, a good time in common to be born, the best time to mate may vary greatly. Small mammals have short gestations (e.g. 21 days for a mouse), and so small mammals begin to mate in the spring and may have several litters before reproduction shuts down as days become shorter in autumn. By contrast, the short-day signals that switch off some small mammals, tend to switch on larger mammals, such as deer. For the does and hinds to produce a fawn or calf in summer, it is necessary to have mated the previous autumn. Foxes also mate early in the year, usually in January and February.

For some species there may be other factors dictating when it is best to mate, and that may require additional adjustments. For example, most female Badgers mate in late spring or early summer, a month or so after they have given birth. But without some additional features this would result in the birth of the next litter cubs in the driest part of the year, a time not greatly enjoyed by Badgers. So to prevent this, the eggs fertilised in the spring float dormant in the mother's uterus until about Christmas when they begin to develop. This means the next litter is delivered on time, late the following spring. Several other species such as seals, Stoats and Pine Martens show this delayed implantation. Bats solve the problem in yet a different manner. They mostly mate in autumn but the females store the sperm and use it to fertilise their eggs when they emerge from hibernation in the spring. Nature has indeed invented an impressive variety of strategies by which mammals cope with living and breeding in spite of the conditions a seasonal climate throws at them.

BIRDS

For birds, having the ability to fly allows more flexibility to survive the changing seasons, with many species undertaking migrations. Spring is a time of great activity, as resident species begin to establish suitable breeding territories. For some this may involve pitched battles for good nest sites but for most, territories are established by flight displays and song. It is for that reason that spring marks the time when birds begin to sing. Birds sing for three reasons. Firstly, it is a non-confrontational method of proclaiming ownership of a territory. It is the males that lay claim to, and defend, territories so usually only males sing. Secondly, it is a way of attracting a female. Thirdly, it is a way for a male bird to inform all of his neighbours that he is still alive. Each bird in an area knows the exact song of its neighbours. When one sings, the others listen and then respond with their own songs. Each song is slightly different from the next. By singing at dawn and at dusk, the birds inform their neighbours that they have survived another night and day — and the status quo remains. However, should one of the birds not sing, this sends out a very different message. The other birds will quickly realise that one of the neighbouring males is gone and will immediately invade that territory in order to extend their own.

Birds also undergo a partial moult in spring, replacing many head and body feathers. This gives most birds a beautiful summer plumage and explains why many of our resident birds appear in pristine condition by April. As well as having a strong song, males also need to look their best to impress the females — their chance of successful breeding depends on it.

For many species, spring is a time of movement when birds that have wintered in Ireland begin to move north to their breeding grounds and when we see the first arrival of our summer visitors. Spring migration (or more correctly, return migration) differs significantly from that of autumn. Birds have a sense of urgency to return to the breeding grounds and the spring journey can sometimes take as little as half to two-thirds the time taken to complete the outward autumn journey. The returning birds all have the experience of completing at least one previous migration.

During the early weeks of spring the first of our migrants arrive along a broad front on our southern coasts. The arrival of spring migrants into Ireland is a staggered one, with birds arriving in 'waves'. As they arrive, the birds slowly work their way up the coasts and inland. The northward surge continues until, like a pincer movement, migrant birds are found along all coastal counties while inland areas are teeming with new arrivals. By late spring our summer migrants will be establishing territories, and native bird song is enhanced by those of our summer visitors. With territories secured, and breeding pairs formed, all birds prepare for the nesting season ahead.

Come early summer our resident and migrant birds are very busy with the pressures of the breeding season. There is still a dawn chorus, but by mid-summer it is only a brief burst of song. Birds employ many different tactics in their nesting strategy but it is important to remember that nests are a purely summer residence for birds — once the breeding season is over the nests are no longer required and are abandoned. Nests vary from simple hollows scraped in the ground like those of terns to highly elaborate and beautiful constructions such as those of Long-tailed Tits. Others nest in holes while species such as Guillemots simply lay their eggs on the ledges of the steepest cliffs. There is no attempt even to build a nest. Other seabirds like Gannets nest on similar steep cliffs but do construct a large, cup-shaped nest of seaweed and other coastal material including discarded fishing netting. These birds rely on the fact that their nests are on such steep cliffs for protection. Potential predators simply cannot reach them.

Many birds of prey nest on ledges of cliffs but will also use old, abandoned Raven nests or even holes in trees. Other birds choose to nest on the ground and use many different strategies for nesting. Some, such as terns, nest in the safety of large colonies while others, like Corncrakes, rely on camouflage to protect their nest location. When they leave the nest, their eggs and chicks are also perfectly camouflaged.

With chicks begging to be fed constantly, adult birds are working flat out from dawn to dusk throughout the summer months. There comes a time when the chicks will leave the nest. The timing of this depends totally on the species involved. For many water birds such as swans and ducks, this happens within hours of hatching. By contrast most small birds leave the nest in two or three weeks while many larger birds can take up to two months or longer. Once they leave the nest, the young birds will usually disperse to different areas within the parents' territory.

For many species, once all of the chicks are fully independent, they will begin the whole process again, attempting to have two or three broods in a season. Others such as Blue Tits will invest all their energies into raising just one large brood. When that brood is successfully fledged they have fulfilled their parental duty for another year. For many species, late summer is also a time for the adults to grow a whole new set of feathers. This post-nuptial moult will replace their old feathers that have been damaged during their breeding season.

Once fledged, young birds must rely on what they have learned in order to survive. Some are only six weeks old or less when they face the world alone. They must be able to fend for themselves, find enough food to survive, be aware of dangers and be strong enough to escape when danger threatens. For species that migrate, they may need to build up enough fat reserves for long flights ahead and, for many young migrant birds, they face the dangers of those long migrations without the assistance of adults. For non-migratory birds, they are facing a winter when food may be scarce and weather may be severe. It is no wonder that the mortality rate for many young birds is so high. All young birds face many tough challenges in their first months on this earth. Only the strongest survive. That any survive at all is remarkable.

As summer turns to early autumn, millions of birds are on the move. Ireland becomes a virtual avian airport. Departing on long-haul flights are birds such as Swallows journeying to far-off destinations such as southern Africa, while warblers may be taking shorter flights to the Mediterranean Basin. In the arrivals lounge are waders, migrating from northern Europe and the Arctic tundra. The transit lounge is also full, with many species simply stopping off in

Ireland en-route to other destinations. For the resident birds and visitors it is a time to prepare for the winter ahead.

There are many differences between spring and autumn migration. The obvious one is the general direction in which the birds are travelling. In spring it is roughly a south-north movement. In autumn it is generally a north-south one. Another big difference is the sheer number of birds on the move. In autumn this involves all the adult migrant birds that have survived the summer and all of their surviving offspring. The third difference is that as so many of the migrating birds are young birds making the journey for the first time, the possibilities of them getting lost is more likely than in spring when returning birds have at least one migration 'under their belt'. Finally, the other major factor is weather. In autumn migrating birds face far more unpredictable and extreme weather systems than they might in spring.

As the winter season progresses the number of returning waders increases. Many will stay for the winter; many more are simply moving through. Among them it is also possible to find waders that have flown at high altitude across the Atlantic Ocean. It is also a time when the southward movements of seabirds takes place off our coasts. Most of our European breeding seabirds winter in the Atlantic and migrate south many kilometres out to sea. However, in certain weather conditions these birds get blown closer to shore and can be seen from headlands and islands.

Birds such as warblers that have bred in Ireland usually work their way south and depart from the most southern headlands and islands. Should we experience strong Atlantic gales there is a possibility of finding American songbirds or even herons that are blown across to Europe.

Autumn migration is a truly breath-taking natural event. It is one of the greatest spectacles on earth and has fascinated humans for thousands of years.

As already mentioned, Ireland's climate, dominated by the mild Atlantic weather systems, means we rarely suffer the harsh winter weather that grips our European neighbours each year. For birds, our comparatively mild winters provide rich, soft feeding for thousands of waders, while our wet climate creates the necessary wetlands for countless wildfowl. As well as that, our relatively snow-free weather provides ideal wintering grounds for migrant thrushes and finches, while our resident species enjoy a lower winter mortality rate than those on mainland Europe. Also, lying on the western edge of Europe, Ireland is ideally located to attract waders, wildfowl and songbirds from breeding grounds in Arctic Canada, Greenland, Iceland, northern Europe and Siberia.

Birds struggle in winter and species employ a wide range of different approaches in order to survive. In autumn many go through a complete moult, giving them new (and sometimes more) feathers to combat the cold while extra fat, put on in late autumn, means that many birds can weigh as much as one-third more in winter than they do in summer. In order to maintain this weight during the winter, small birds may need to eat as much as one-quarter of their body weight each day to survive, and spend from dawn to dusk searching for food. Water is also essential, particularly during cold snaps, when, as well as needing to drink, birds need to wash and preen to keep those all-important, insulating feathers in perfect condition.

In winter Irish birds perform mini-migrations, and many species engage in altitudinal migration (they leave the higher, colder areas to winter on the lowlands or along the coast). If the weather turns cold many woodland species move out of their usual habitats in search of food and find their way into gardens, attracted by the regular food supply. In other species, females, weighing less than males and therefore less capable of storing enough fat reserves to see them through a hard winter, fly south to France, leaving a 'male only' population behind, defending their territories.

As winter takes hold in Europe, birds begin to move westwards in an attempt both to avoid the weather and to find food. Each winter Blackbirds, Mistle Thrushes along with Redwings and Fieldfares migrate to Ireland in hundreds of thousands, with equally large numbers of finches including Chaffinches, Siskins and Bramblings. For birds, winter can be a tough time but our rich food supply and the diversity of our native habitats ensures that enough birds survive to either breed again in Ireland or migrate back to their northern breeding grounds.

The changing seasons have a profound impact on all our flora and fauna, both resident and migratory. That each species can breed, feed and survive the challenges that each season presents, is proof of just how highly evolved and adaptable they truly are.

Eric Dempsey
Declan Doogue
Tom Hayden

Spring

Red Fox

Vulpes vulpes
Sionnach/madra rua

There is probably no mammal in Ireland that more emphasises the urban-rural divide than the Fox. While the Red Fox treats urban and rural habitats alike as desirable places to live, the humans who cohabit with it are not so unanimous. Urban dwellers in general are enchanted by a glimpse of a Red Fox as it goes about its nightly business. To see a Red Fox at or after dusk trotting leisurely through its territory that it knows so well is to experience a handsome beast apparently at ease with its environment. In urban areas Red Foxes, who will eat almost anything, are primarily scavengers and hunters secondarily, and they readily incorporate nightly visits to houses where the owners provide them with food. In the country the relationship between foxes and humans is more uneasy. In general they play an important role in controlling rabbits, rats and mice and it is often forgotten that much of their diet consists of earthworms, beetles and a variety of fruits.

But it is their natural tendency to hunt, or more particularly the impression that they indulge in gratuitous killing, that lands Red Foxes in trouble. If they gain access to houses of domestic fowl or the rearing-pens of pheasants, they often engage in surplus killing and cache extra food. This is probably brought about by the excitement and panic in the birds, added to the fact that they have no means of escape. Red Foxes also prey disproportionately on free-ranging domestic fowl or recently released pheasants, creatures that have lost their natural wariness and thus are not equipped for life in the wild. As if this was not enough, their tendency to scavenge carcases of deer, or of small domestic animals such as sheep and lambs, further tarnishes their reputation. Many a Red Fox has been condemned before it was clear whether it had killed a lamb or was feeding on a lamb that had died of other causes.

Red Foxes mate relatively early in the year and their other-worldly triple-bark and eerie screams are a sure sign of wooing foxes. Most mating takes place during January and February and the cubs are born in March and April. Red Foxes are attentive parents, and while the vixen remains with the cubs for almost a month, the dog-fox brings her food to support her lactation. By May or June the cubs are venturing out of the den and beginning to explore their surroundings. By November they will have to leave the den and strike out on their own.

Robin

Erithacus rubecula
Spideog

Blue Tit

Cyanistes caeruleus
Meantán gorm

Long-tailed Tit

Aegithalos caudatus
Meantán earrfhada

As the first signs of spring arrive, resident birds begin to check out suitable breeding sites and territories. Each dawn is greeted with bird song which, as the spring progresses and summer migrants arrive to our shores, reaches its peak in what we refer to as the dawn chorus. By late spring and early summer our parks, towns and woodlands are alive with the sound of bird song. But why do birds sing? Firstly, it is to declare a territory. As males find and defend the territory, it is only the males that sing. Female birds in the northern hemisphere rarely sing. So singing is a non-confrontational method of creating boundaries between two territories. Secondly, it is to attract a mate. Studies have shown that in some species the females can judge the strength of the male and even how good his territory is by the quality of the male's song. Finally, it is to inform your neighbours that you are still alive. Singing at dawn and at dusk is a declaration to your neighbours that you are very much around. Most species do not sing after the breeding season, with the exceptions of Robins. The Robins maintain and hold their territory even in winter so the males sing throughout the entire year. This Blue Tit and Robin were both photographed in the Botanic Gardens, Dublin, while the singing Long-tailed Tit was photographed near Roundwood, Wicklow.

Robin

Long-tailed Tit

Blue Tit

Grey Heron

Ardea cinerea
Corr réisc

Grey Heron is a common and widespread breeding species found along rivers, canals, lakes and wetlands as well as coastal estuaries. They nest in trees in colonies called heronries and construct large, untidy nests of sticks. Each year the nest is re-used and added to so that, in old heronries, the nests can be quite substantial. Feeding on a variety of fish, frogs, insects, birds and even rodents, Grey Herons are renowned for the patient hunting techniques that can see them remain motionless for long periods staring into the water. When they spot a fish, they plunge their dagger-like beak into the water in an instant and grab their prey. The Grey Heron pictured here was fishing in small ponds in the Botanic Gardens, Dublin.

Primrose

Primula vulgaris

Primrose, part ancestor of many garden *Polyanthus*, is one of the most successful occupants of the hedgerow bank. Originally and naturally a plant of woodland margins and clearings, it was once common on roadside hedge banks, safe there from heavy grazing though not from flower pickers. It was adopted as a political emblem by the supporters of Disraeli following his death and was worn in remembrance to the point where at the end of the 19th century botanists had become conscious of its disappearance from sites near Dublin where it had been previously abundant. It hybridises with Cowslip, a plant of lime-rich grasslands, resulting usually in plants with tall stalks and larger flowers arranged in an umbel. To complicate the matter further, some roadside plants seem to be naturally occurring crosses between garden Primulas and wild Primroses, resulting in a number of unusual colour forms.

Lords-and-Ladies

Arum maculatum

Lords-and-Ladies, *Arum maculatum*, should, according to its specific name, have spotted leaves but the plants in Ireland are seldom marked, although they are more widely so in Britain. Its multiplicity of popular names reflects its familiarity to the observer. The pale-green sheathing hood unfurls in spring to reveal a purple-brown spadix, below which the future fruits will form. In the enclosure at the base of the sheath a scent is secreted by the plant which is attractive to insects that are trapped within and released as the sheath withers. It is related to the Altar-lily, better known in Ireland as Easter Lily, another species that has been adopted as a political emblem.

By the end of spring the greenish fruits of Lords-and-Ladies are turning scarlet, providing the only splash of bright colour, and will persist long after the spear-shaped leaves have gone into decay.

Little Egret

Egretta garzetta
Éigrit bheag

Formerly a rare spring and summer vagrant to Ireland, Little Egrets are now a resident, and spreading, breeding species. Nesting in small colonies in trees, they can be found in a variety of habitats, from coastal estuaries and wetlands to inland lakes and rivers. As spring arrives the birds acquire long plumes on the head and elongated feathers on the back and wings called aigrettes. Such ornamental feathers almost caused the birds' extinction in the late 19th century — they were much prized by the fashion industry as adornments for hats. Unlike the patient fishing techniques of Grey Herons, Little Egrets are far more active, running after small fish, using their legs and feet to frighten fish out of cover and opening their wings to cast shadows on the water. This Little Egret was hunting small fish in a pool near Rosscarbery, Cork.

Pine Marten

Martes martes
Cat crainn

In Ireland people fall into two categories, those who would love to see a Pine Marten but never have, and those who see them regularly. The Pine Marten is paradoxically shy and elusive but may become quite tame and accustomed to humans near by. Recently reports are increasing of Pine Martens nesting in attics, much to the alarm of the householders. Pine Martens almost became extinct through the combined effects of deforestation, control by gamekeepers and accidental killing by poison laid to control foxes. Fortunately all three have been almost eliminated and the Pine Marten is recovering and extending its range. Most sightings of Pine Martens are random, but if they are suspected to be in the vicinity they may be enticed to show themselves by establishing feeding stations baited with blackberry or raspberry jam, to which they are extremely partial. The usual first sign of a Pine Marten are its droppings which have a braided appearance and are deposited with a flourish which folds it back on itself sometimes like a doughnut. These droppings are deposited at favoured sites along the edges of forest roads or tracks or on conspicuous earth mounds, rocks or tree trunks.

Pine Martens are about the same size as a domestic cat. They have a rich, thick, dark-brown coat with reddish under-fur and they have a creamy-white patch under the chin and on the throat that makes individuals recognisable. Their tail is long and luxuriant and they have large, mobile, rounded, pale ears. They are extremely agile with large, hairy feet and their claws may be partly retracted, more so than a dog but less than a cat. The Pine Marten flows through trees with such feline grace that its old Irish name was cat crainn (tree cat) and many Irish placenames including cat refer to the Pine Marten.

Pine Martens mate in August and September but the females do not begin gestation for several months, depending on the food and weather. Therefore the birth season may vary from year to year but usually occurs between late March and early May.

The Pine Marten is technically a carnivore but with omnivorous tendencies. It preys on mice, rats, young rabbits, squirrels, frogs, crabs, earthworms, beetles and birds at roost. In autumn it eats blackberries, ivy berries, sloes and mushrooms. It will also scavenge on carrion which makes it susceptible to poisoned bait laid for the control of foxes.

Mountain Avens

Dryas octopetala

Mountain Avens festoons the warm, dry rocks of the Burren in spring, with its dense mats of twiggy, low-growing vegetation, contrasting with the masses of bright white flowers. Biogeographically it is a very interesting species, being essentially a plant of cold climates. It was widespread in boreal times and is still found on cold higher ground in Central Europe as well as being more common on rocky ground farther north. However, it grows comfortably in the Burren and elsewhere on rocky ground, often with species from much warmer climates. Its growth form, hugging the ground, enables it to grow in wind-swept areas and in turn it provides shelter for other smaller and more delicate species.

Shrubby Cinquefoil

Potentilla fruticosa

Shrubby Cinquefoil is more familiar in Ireland as a robust garden plant than as a rare, native low shrub. It is widely planted as part of ornamental surrounds on roundabouts and in parks and occurs in a variety of colour forms. In its typical natural habitat and in its usual yellow flower form it grows on the upper parts of turloughs, the unusual disappearing lakes of the Burren and elsewhere. It also occurs in a few areas in Northern England but after that must be sought in colder climes. This indicates the difficulty that certain species have in spreading beyond their preferred natural habitats. There is a profound difference between growing for a number of years where planted in gardens and growing naturally as an on-going, reproducing, self-sustaining colony without the agency of humankind.

Mountain Avens

Shrubby Cinquefoil

Black Medick

Medicago lupulina

Black Medick is a member of the clover family, many of which (including White Clover, *Trifolium repens*, Red Clover, *Trifolium pratense*, and Lesser Trefoil, *Trifolium dubium*), at various stages have been pressed to do duty as 'shamrock'. Most of the commercial product nowadays is *Trifolium dubium*, which if left to its own devices would come into flower in early May when it produces a tiny cluster of yellow flowers very similar to Black Medick. The leaves of the two species are very different, however, with the tip of the leaves of the medick bearing a minute point which is actually the central vein protruding slightly. Common Trefoil lacks this feature, is less robust and lacks the obvious hairs of medick. Both species are common on sunny, lime-rich soils on roadsides, the medick having the slight advantage on more disturbed ground in built-up environments.

Blackthorn

Prunus spinosa

Blackthorn, the raw material for the celebrated or infamous blackthorn stick, forms a tough, solid stem, often armed with sharp spines. It flowers early in the year, usually well before the leaves appear. In autumn it produces the familiar fruit known as sloes, used to enhance (or disguise?) the taste of gin. Blackthorn can also spread by suckering and can often be seen spreading out into fields where grazing has been reduced or abandoned. Though usually encountered as an erect shrub, it also grows more or less prostrate, especially in areas exposed to the wind. Once rooted and established, it can cling to the ground, conforming to the contours of the soil and exposed rock.

Little Grebe

Tachybaptus ruficollis
Spágaire tonn

The smallest and most widespread members of the grebe family, Little Grebes are found on lakes, ponds, wetlands and rivers in all regions. In winter they can also be found in estuary channels and harbours. As spring arrives the birds change from their pale, drab winter plumage and show the rich chestnut colours on the head as this bird is showing. They build floating nests made of aquatic vegetation placed among reeds and sedges, and the young leave the nest within hours of hatching. The adults make very good parents and will frequently carry the young on their backs. They feed on a variety of tiny fish, insects, insect larvae and molluscs. This bird was fishing along the River Dodder, Dublin.

Bluebells

Hyacinthoides non-scripta

Bluebells are resilient elements of the woodland flora and can grow in both acid and lime-rich conditions. They can even survive in densely planted conifer woodlands — at least on their margins. Many of our bluebells are not the true native species, but are garden ejects, thrown over the cottage-garden wall to flourish with equal success on roadside verges, an unfortunate characteristic held in common with many other over-successful garden plants. The main ejectees are Spanish Bluebells, *Hyacinthoides hispanica*. These differ from our native bluebell in having an inflorescence with flowers all around the stem, in contrast to the Irish one which has a smaller number of flowers, confined mainly to one side. The stem of the native plant therefore tilts to one side whilst that of the garden plants is held more erect. There are other differences in the flowers. In woodlands that have been gardened, the two species come into contact and form disconcertingly large numbers of hybrids. It appears that these hybrids may be more common than has been previously suspected and like many other undesirable garden plants may be increasing at the (genetic) expense of our native species. Furthermore, it is suspected that many of the plants expelled from gardens are themselves hybrids.

Bluebells

Grey Partridge

Perdix perdix
Patraisc

Formerly a scarce but widespread resident breeding species, the Irish Grey Partridge population declined drastically as a result of habitat loss. Found on bogs and moorlands, near grain crops and rough pastures, the species was confined to just one area in the midlands. By the turn of the 20th century the population of Grey Partridges in Ireland was down to little more than ten individuals. However, a re-introduction programme involving birds from central Europe as well as habitat protection measures has resulted in a slight increase in the population during the first decade of the 21st century. This male, hiding in dense cover, was holding territory and engaging in courtship displays with a female at the Lough Boora Parklands, Offaly.

Spring Gentian

Gentiana verna

Bird's-foot Trefoil

Lotus corniculatus

The striking blue flowers of Spring Gentian contrast with the yellow of Bird's-foot Trefoil. The Gentian is widespread on exposed limestone rocks in the west of Ireland and flowers abundantly in spring. It is one of a group of species more typical of colder climates, not a true alpine, but often appearing in alpine gardens. In Ireland, along with a few other species, it exhibits an anomalous community ecology, growing cheek by jowl with several species from southern Europe from very different habitats. In contrast, Bird's-foot Trefoil is widespread, growing on stabilised limestone grassland found inland and more securely on sand-dunes and grassland in esker country.

Common Frog

Rana temporaria
Frog/Loscann

For creatures that cannot control their body temperatures, Common Frogs can be extremely active early in the year. While they spend the coldest period of mid-winter hibernating they are among the earliest of our terrestrial vertebrates to breed in the year. Breeding takes place between February and April. They use a range of hibernating sites, piles of decaying vegetation, compost heaps or the mud and roots at the bottom of ponds; but with the increase in day-length after mid-winter they begin to prepare for breeding. Once the temperature rises above five degrees, adult frogs are ready to breed. Male frogs arrive at or near the site where they were born, detecting it partly by the scent of algae in the water. These will provide food for the developing tadpoles. As soon as males arrive at a breeding site they begin croaking to attract females and to threaten other males.

Common Frogs are 'explosive breeders' in every sense. They breed once a year and a female may produce between 1,000 and 2,000 eggs, losing up to a third of her body weight in the process. While the female has some control of breeding, in that she chooses the location at which she will spawn, in practice breeding is rather chaotic. Indeed sometimes males attempt to mate with other males in the confusion. The breeding female is grabbed by the smaller male, and when the eggs are shed he releases his sperm over them. However, since fertilisation is external, other pirate males may also release their sperm into the mix, and while the tadpoles that hatch from a clump of spawn have the same mother, many of them will be half siblings because several males may have succeeded in fertilising some of the eggs. Fertilised eggs sink briefly as a protective coat forms over them, and when this jelly absorbs water the egg mass rises to the surface. Eggs at the surface are less prone to chilling than those deeper in the water.

Often many masses of eggs may come together in a large aggregation. This has several advantages. Firstly, the anonymity of the crowd protects individual eggs. Secondly, such a large mass of developing eggs generates small amounts of heat that keeps the water marginally warmer than if they were dispersed.

Ramsons

Allium ursinum

Ramsons is mentioned in ancient Gaelic literature and is certainly not a plant likely to be missed in springtime. It can form huge stands in native woodlands, often to the exclusion of most other species. It is a member of the garlic family and its leaves release a scent that can be detected at some distance. It can persist in some hedgerows long after the adjoining woodland has been cleared, providing enduring evidence of the presence of former woodland. Indeed it can even survive in situations where the original woodland has been cleared and re-planted with exotic, non-native flowers and trees. A close relative, Three-cornered Garlic, *Allium triquetrum*, with taller, very three-angled stems, is now becoming a major pest on roadside verges in many parts of Ireland. It is another of the many garden plants that have escaped onto semi-natural ground at the expense of the native flora.

Lapwing

Vanellus vanellus
Pilibín

A widespread breeding species found on wetlands and grasslands, Lapwing populations have decreased in recent years due to habitat loss. Nesting in a simple scrape in the ground makes them very susceptible to disturbance and predation. In winter our population increases with the arrival of birds from Europe. By spring, Irish Lapwings which may have wintered at coastal locations return to their breeding grounds. By then the birds are showing their full, glossy summer plumage and their long crests which are longer on males than on females. This adult male was patrolling his established territory in the Lough Boora Parklands, Offaly. He was also engaged in buoyant flight displays to declare and defend his territory from rival males as well as to impress potential mates.

Feral Goat

Capra hircus
Gabhar fiáin

One of the most surprising experiences in the Irish countryside is to encounter a newborn Feral Goat kid in the depths of January. This timing seems so inappropriate to Ireland's climate. Deer, for example, give birth mainly in May and June. Surely the cold and wet weather should be too much for such kids and natural selection would have eliminated early breeding from the population? There may be two reasons why this has not happened. Firstly, although the weather in January may be cold and wet, the following months are not much better. Secondly, events in the history of the goat have made it hardy enough to withstand such an unpromising start. The reward for such resilience is that early breeding offers early maturity for the kids, and many early-born kids mate the following autumn and give birth themselves on their first birthday.

The long association between goats and humans may in part account for their early breeding and hardiness. It seems that Ireland's original goats were a type that was selected to thrive around the northern and western margins of Europe at a time when the climate was much colder and the northern glaciers extended much further south than they do now. Ireland's Feral Goat herds contain a mixture of individuals with a long family history of living wild, together with individuals descended from improved dairy breeds and who were released or abandoned by their owners in more recent times. There is a need to identify individuals of the old Irish type and conserve them before they disappear through crossing with individuals of the modern type.

Both billies and nannies bear curved horns that grow throughout life. The external sheath, that covers the bony core within, shows seasonal differences in growth rate, and the age of the animal can be estimated by the number of winter phases of growth.

If Feral Goats are encountered, their reaction differs greatly from that of deer. Not for them a headlong dash to a safer distance. They move calmly, relatively slowly and unobtrusively and can cover surprisingly long distances with little effort. This makes attempts to round up Feral Goats particularly frustrating and it is quite difficult to approach them closely unless care is taken to avoid alarming them unduly.

This kid, photographed in Glendalough, was trying to suckle every few minutes. It had evidently been born earlier that day.

Black Guillemot

Cepphus grylle
Foracha dhubh

While many birds declare their territories in non-confrontational ways such as singing, other species engage in open conflict with the approach of the breeding season. Some, such as seabirds, breed in colonies where nesting sites are at a premium. These may be simply narrow pieces of cliff edge or, for others, perhaps a nesting burrow. Black Guillemots nest under boulders on seacliffs but also use crevices in pier walls. At Gyles Quay in Louth, tunnels have been inserted in the pier specially for breeding Black Guillemots. In spring such pieces of prime Black Guillemot real estate are highly prized and rival males will engage in prolonged fights to secure one. These birds were fighting for over 20 minutes inside the harbour at Gyles Quay before moving out to sea where the battle continued for another 15 minutes. Eventually one of the birds broke away from the conflict and flew farther out to sea. The winning male returned to claim his chosen nesting site.

Sedge Warbler

Acrocephalus schoenobaenus
Ceolaire cíbe

Sedge Warblers are a common and widespread summer visitor from their wintering grounds in southern Africa and are found in a wide range of habitats — reed-beds, marshes, sedges and bushes close to water. Males arrive on the breeding grounds first and proclaim their territories by singing and engaging in short flight displays. They are renowned for their improvised, scratchy songs that never include the same complete phrase twice. When each phrase of a song is finished, they start the next section with the notes that ended the previous one. It seems that no two Sedge Warblers sing the same song and, as well as this, they also mimic other bird sounds, incorporating these into their own songs. This bird was photographed at Tacumshin Lake, Wexford.

Hazel

Corylus avellana

The female flowers of Hazel are often the first to appear in spring or even late winter. They are very small and likely to be missed unless searched for. They are basically little more than a cluster of reddish stigmas, held in place by bud-like scales, that will be pollinated by clouds of pollen released by the nearby, more obvious male catkins, dangling and yellow in appearance. Later in the year they will produce the familiar hazel nuts. In some areas Hazel is recolonising abandoned rocky grassland from where it had been ousted by grazing. Outside its optimal area it often occurs in hedgerows, sometimes with other species typical of limestone scrub and in these circumstances may indicate the presence of former native woodland. It usually does not form a tall central trunk but rather produces separate woody stems eminently suitable as poles for fencing, wattles and broom handles.

Mediterranean Gull

Larus melanocephalus
Sléibhín Meánmhuirí

This handsome gull species was once a very rare vagrant to Ireland from southern Europe. However, during the 1980s Mediterranean Gulls began to expand their breeding range farther north and the species became a regular, annual visitor. By the end of the 20th century the species was breeding in small numbers in Ireland, and each winter sees the arrival of hundreds of birds from Europe. The wintering birds remain until early spring before they return to their respective breeding grounds. However, before they leave, many adults moult into their full, hooded, breeding plumage. This superb adult Mediterranean Gull was photographed at Sandycove, Dublin.

Wild Strawberry

Fragaria vesca

Wild Strawberry grows on the margins of woodlands, on hedge banks and even in ungrazed, rocky grassland. It produces small, very tasty strawberries in early summer. Its flowers are considerably larger than the superficially similar Barren Strawberry, *Potentilla sterilis*. The latter species produces a dry fruit. When in flower, the petals of Wild Strawberry are overlapping while the petals of Barren Strawberry (which is a much earlier flowerer) are clearly separated from each other.

Grey Squirrel

Sciurus carolinensis
Iora glas

In January and February a commotion in the canopy of deciduous trees in an urban park is often due to the mating chases of Grey Squirrels. These can be quite hectic, noisy and protracted. Although extremely acrobatic in the trees, Grey Squirrels spend considerable periods on the ground and so are quite easily observed, a fact that accounts in part for their popularity.

An individual Grey Squirrel is a most engaging and resourceful rogue but collectively they are one of Ireland's most destructive, invasive mammals. Grey squirrels evolved in the deciduous woodlands of eastern North America. Therefore they have found Ireland's deciduous woodlands and urban parks much to their liking; so much so, that from a nucleus of less than 10 individuals, misguidedly released as a wedding present in 1911, they spread from County Longford and now are found in 26 of the 32 counties. In the course of their relentless progress they have come into contact with the native Red Squirrel. The Red Squirrel had evolved as a creature of the pine forests in Eurasia but in the absence of a competitor was able to maintain itself in deciduous and mixed woodland. However, with the arrival of the Grey Squirrel who was better adapted to deciduous woods, the Red Squirrel began to disappear. This is due to a number of factors. Firstly, Grey Squirrels are better able to deal with acorns before these are ripe enough for Red Squirrels and so deplete this food source first. Secondly, Grey Squirrels carry a parapox virus that evolved with them and to which they, unlike the Red Squirrels, are relatively immune. Red Squirrels are at serious risk and will continue to be so unless and until they or the virus mutates such that they become more resistant or it becomes less virulent. Thirdly, Grey Squirrels are considerably larger (by 30–50 per cent) than Red Squirrels.

Grey Squirrels are particularly destructive to many species of trees, particularly maples. They live mainly on seeds and fruit in winter and spring which they may store in caches for later consumption. They eat acorns, beech mast, hazelnuts and pine seeds. In summer and autumn they switch to buds, flowers and bark. In particular they have a great fondness for sugary sap and they strip the bark off trees to get at it. If the bark stripping is severe enough, it may kill the tree. Grey Squirrels are active by day, all year round. They do not hibernate but in extreme weather they may spend several days inside their dreys, roughly spherical nests of twigs and leaves, constructed in a forked branch of a tree.

(Eric Dempsey)

Irish Hare

Lepus timidus
Giorria

Everywhere else where it occurs, the Irish Hare is termed the Mountain Hare because it is only found at high altitudes or at high latitudes. But in Ireland it is found at all altitudes from sea level to the tops of our highest mountains. It has evolved as a creature of open habitats such as coastal grassland, agricultural pasture or upland moors. Part of its survival strategy is to rely on speed and stamina to escape danger, unlike its cousin the Rabbit which never strays far from cover and sprints to a secure burrow when alarmed. There has been an unfortunate consequence of the hand that evolution has dealt to the Irish Hare: its habits have rendered it suitable for coursing with dogs.

When Irish Hares moult in autumn, the reddish-brown summer coat is usually replaced by a greyish-brown one. Elsewhere, where winter snow cover is prolonged, Mountain Hares grow a white winter coat. Irish Hares almost certainly also turned white in winter soon after the last ice age when winters were more severe. But in the meantime natural selection has almost, but not entirely, removed the genes for colour change from the Irish population. White or partially white hares can occasionally be seen around the country in winter.

Irish Hares feed on a variety of plants such as grasses, herbs and heathers. They will also browse on willow, gorse, bilberry and other shrubs. They pass their food through their gut twice. They do not produce faeces by day, but rather a semi-digested bolus of plant material that they swallow and send through the digestive process again. The second time it emerges, at night, it is in the form of hard pellets that are deposited. Hares tend to be more active by night, foraging in one location, and they rest elsewhere by day in special nests called forms. During the breeding season (January to October), however, Irish Hares may be active by day and night. The heightened activity has led to the notion of the Mad March Hares. During courtship the female may squabble with one or more males who may in turn fight with one another, by boxing or kicking, in between protracted chases.

After a pregnancy lasting about seven weeks, a litter of usually two or three leverets, fully furred and with eyes open, are born in the form. They remain largely alone in the form for the first few days, and are usually only visited by their mother to feed them at dusk. After about one week they are more mobile and are weaned after three.

Germander Speedwell

Veronica chamaedrys

Germander Speedwell is widespread on woodland margins and hedge banks and can even grow in lawns and grasslands on slightly deeper soils. It has a very simple flower, four petals, two stamens and a protruding stigma and style, a feature shared with many native and weedy speedwells as well as the so-called garden 'Veronicas' — (Hebe). Wood Speedwell, *Veronica montana*, is similar, but has paler green leaves and more lilac-coloured petals. It is common in deciduous woodlands on limestone soils. One of the most notorious of lawn weeds, Creeping Speedwell, *Veronica filiformis*, forms great patches in lawns with bright-blue petals in spring. It has bright blue flowers and when it dies back it leaves bare patches on the lawn. It was brought into Ireland as a garden plant, one of many that are now threatening our native flora. Although it rarely if ever produces seeds in this country, it seems to have little difficulty in spreading vegetatively into areas where it is definitely not a desideratum.

Jackdaw

Corvus monedula
Cág

One of our more familiar and common members of the crow family, Jackdaws are found in towns, cities, parks, farmlands and woodlands. In winter the birds can form large flocks and join other crow species such as Rooks. In summer they breed in loose colonies and build nests of twigs in holes in trees, cliffs, quarries and old derelict buildings. Another favourite nesting location is inside chimneys, regardless of whether the house is derelict or occupied. In many areas, people place small metal grids over the chimneys to prevent the birds from constructing their nests inside. In this house the owners placed chicken wire over the chimney in an attempt to stop the birds. But being a highly intelligent species, this pair simply pulled the wire back from the chimney entrance and began nesting. These Jackdaws were photographed in the grounds of Coolure House, Westmeath.

Woodpigeon

Columba palumbus
Colm coille

Our largest pigeon species, Woodpigeons are an extremely common species found in woodlands, towns, parks, gardens and farmlands. They are best distinguished from other similar pigeons and doves by their size and striking, white neck-collars. They feed on a variety of seeds, cereals and insects but will also eat young shoots which makes them unpopular with some farmers and gardeners. They build large, flimsy nests in trees and hedges. The parents feed their young on 'pigeon milk' which is a secretion from their crop. In summer the males engage in flight displays involving steep upwards flights during which the birds clap their wings together. This is followed by long, downward glides. When seen in good light, the subtle purple and green sheen to the birds' neck feathers makes them a very striking and colourful bird. This splendid bird was feeding among early spring flowers in the Botanic Gardens, Dublin.

Giant Horsetail

Equisetum telmateia

Golden Saxifrage

Chrysosplenium oppositifolium

Giant Horsetail is a large relation of the familiar garden pest Field Horsetail, *Equisetum arvense*, which is proving so difficult to eradicate. In spring it produces large cones, 4cm or more long. These grow rapidly on pale, brown-ringed stems and in less than a few weeks will have produced and released their spores, and decayed. However, at the same time the plant produces large, non-fertile stems often almost a metre tall with ivory-white stems and rings of green, narrow branches. Giant Horsetail is usually found in association with springs and seepage lines, especially in lime-rich districts. Usually other uncommon species grow nearby, slightly upslope. One of these is Golden Saxifrage which covers very wet mud in damp woodlands. In these shaded areas, lime is often washed out of the adjoining soils, percolating down the slopes, becoming deposited like limescale on leaves, twigs and fallen trees. In dry summers, when the surplus water has disappeared, the ground is much firmer here and the soil and fallen vegetation in these areas appears whitish, as if dusted with natural cement.

Whimbrel

Numenius phaeopus
Crotach eanaigh

Whimbrels are a common spring and autumn passage migrant, occurring in Ireland as the birds move to and from their breeding grounds in Iceland and northern Europe. Wintering in Africa, they are often among the first spring migrants to arrive on coastal wetlands, estuaries and mudflats. They resemble Curlews but are smaller, show shorter bills and have distinctive stripes on their heads. During migration they are very vocal, giving fast, rolling, whistling calls to keep in touch with each other as they fly in small flocks. By mid-May most birds will have moved through Ireland and it will be early autumn before the birds are seen again. This small group was photographed as they flew in off the sea to land on the beach at Gormanstown, Meath.

Willow Warbler

Phylloscopus trochilus
Ceolaire sailí

Willow Warblers are a very common and widespread summer visitor from wintering grounds that stretch from just south of the Sahara Desert to southern Africa. Found in woodlands, bushes, hedgerows and copses, the clear, descending notes of their song is a true sound of spring. They feed on a variety of insects and spiders which are either delicately picked off leaves and branches, or skilfully caught during brief aerial pursuits. Willow Warblers build domed nests on or just above the ground, usually well concealed in dense vegetation. This bird was photographed in woodlands near Kenmare, Kerry.

Dog-violets

Viola riviniana, Viola reichenbachiana

In spring most hedges on lime-rich soils will have colonies of Common Dog-violet, *Viola riviniana*. Typically this species has a white spur and overlapping petals. Older hedges and native woodland will occasionally have the rarer Early Dog-violet, *Viola reichenbachiana*, with a dark spur and non-overlapping petals. Both species have a fairly evident leaf-rosette, which in woodlands opens out above the mat of leaf litter that has persisted from the preceding autumn. Many of the hedgerow violets in Ireland are slightly intermediate in character. Both species can grow in woodlands, often with Wood Sanicle, *Sanicula europaea*, and Barren Strawberry, *Potentilla sterilis*. The Heath Dog-violet, *Viola canina*, is a much rarer plant of leached sand-dunes and rocky lakeshores with a much more yellow spur and no obvious rosette.

Common Tern

Sterna hirundo
Geabhróg

Common Terns are, as their name suggests, a common and widespread summer visitor from their wintering grounds off West Africa. Found on coastal and inland lake islands, the birds nest on the ground in large colonies often containing other species such as Sandwich and Arctic Terns. Returning to Ireland by early April, they first appear along southern coastal areas before gradually working their way back into their breeding grounds. Like other tern species, Common Terns feed on a variety of fish which are caught by first hovering over the water, locating their prey by sight and then diving headfirst into the water. When fishing, the birds show great aerial skills, concentration and flexibility as they manoeuvre into position before each dive. This Common Tern was photographed fishing off Gormanstown Beach, Meath.

Ground Ivy

Glechoma hederacea

Ground Ivy is one of the first plants to flower in hedgerows, often long before much larger species get into their stride. An herbaceous perennial, it flowers early, producing small clumps of blue-tubed flowers coming directly off the stem. It is a relative of the larger-flowered dead-nettles (*Lamium*) and a large range of garden flowers and herbs. In common with many hedgerow species it is essentially a woodland-margin plant, able to extend its range along the network of field boundaries and roadside verges. Here it is more protected from grazing. However, as the season advances, it tends to become engulfed by taller-growing species such as Hogweed and Cow Parsley.

Dandelion

Taraxacum

Dandelions are some of the first plants to flower in spring. There are many species of true dandelion in Ireland and many more to be discovered, as our knowledge of this critical and difficult group improves. Most of the early-flowering species are associated with weedy conditions such as urban and waste-ground sites. They grow well in parks, ironically where weed killers have been applied in the previous year, and also thrive on motorway verges. As the year advances, other native species come into flower. Lightly shaded roadside banks, damp grassland, sand-dunes and lake shores are favoured habitats where many rare species occur. Even in urban habitats a wide variety of species can be encountered. Long before they come into flower, differences are obvious in the degree and character of the indentation of leaves, in the presence or absence of spots and blotches and later in the size of the flowering heads and colour of the outer bracts. Each dandelion head is an amalgamation of many separate flowers, from which the individual fruits (achenes) develop. Each successful achene is surmounted by a parachute (pappus). When the achene is mature and the pappus dry, these will be blown away to colonise new, open ground. In the past dandelions were used to make dandelion wine (flowers), salads (leaves) and a coffee substitute (roots).

Water Crowfoot

Ranunculus

The splendid flowers of several species of Water Crowfoot (members of the Buttercup family), held above the water, add a spectacular layer of colour to Irish river and lake surfaces from late spring onwards. Some species have floating, three-lobed leaves, some have totally submerged, thread-like leaves and some have combinations of both types. Many of the large-flowered species have been ousted from their riverine habitats by water pollution and have been replaced by more aggressive pondweeds (*Potamogeton*) tolerant of more eutrophic conditions. Other smaller species are better able to tolerate high nutrient conditions and some can even flower and fruit on almost dry, cattle-trodden mud.

Hedgehog

Erinaceus europaeus
Gráinneog

Hedgehogs are the harbingers of spring. They spend the winter, from about November until March or April, hibernating in special nests made of leaves or grass in sheltered locations. Nevertheless, during this time they are quite sensitive to their surroundings. Although their heart rate may have decreased from about 200 to 20 per minute and their body temperature may be as low as five degrees, nevertheless if the temperature approaches zero, they use special brown fat to generate heat and warm themselves to avoid freezing to death. They also wake up occasionally to urinate and may even venture out or change nests if the weather is mild enough.

When hedgehogs finally emerge from hibernation they are usually quite thin, having lost almost half their body weight, mostly fat, during the winter. They have two priorities — to satisfy their enormous appetites and to find a mate. They are nocturnal and will eat almost anything they can catch, such as slugs, beetles, earthworms, caterpillars, earwigs, millipedes, fruit, berries, birds' eggs, small mammals and even carrion. A hedgehog munching through a slug is a surprisingly noisy activity. Hedgehogs are not particularly territorial and live mostly solitary lives. If a group should be observed, it is usually either a number of individuals that have been attracted to the same food source or else a group in search of a mating opportunity. Breeding takes place between May and October. A male and female spend little time together beyond the duration of the courtship and mating. The old joke about hedgehogs mating carefully is true. Courtship is a noisy affair and involves much chasing of the female by the male and mutual circling of one another until the female finally decides to accept her suitor and rearranges her spines to accommodate him. They then go their separate ways. But fidelity is not high on a hedgehog's list of priorities; many females mate with more than one male and in many litters the young hedgehogs are a mixture of full and half siblings.

Hedgehogs can move surprisingly rapidly and their legs are longer than most people imagine. They emit wheezy, snorting sounds as they forage for food. They hiss and may scream or erect their spines when threatened. If the threat is more severe they roll into a ball. They have a muscle that acts like a drawstring that pulls the spiny skin such that the hedgehog is enclosed within a prickly purse. This deters most predators, except badgers who are able to kill hedgehogs and turn the skin inside-out despite the spines.

Lesser Celandine

Lesser Celandine

Ficaria verna

Lesser Celandine (pages 64–5) is one of the first species to poke up through the leaf litter. It over-winters underground as little clusters of tubers and is therefore ready to grow as soon as soil temperatures rise sufficiently. Once started, it develops rapidly and can flower within a few weeks, sometimes covering the ground in great yellow sheets. There are two separate subspecies known from Ireland. One, more common in natural woodlands, has a flower-head of overlapping petals and produces seed heads with twenty or more achenes. The other subspecies, sometimes growing as a garden weed, has fewer non-overlapping petals and produces seed heads with only a few developed achenes. Towards the end of spring this subspecies produces small, pale, cigar-shaped tubers growing in the join of leaf and stem. As the plant decomposes these fall to the ground and can often be seen exposed on the surface of the soil when the parent plant has completely disappeared. These tubers will in turn form new plants in the following spring.

Hawthorn

Crataegus monogyna

Hawthorn is usually encountered as a hedgerow shrub, where it has been widely planted. It has many properties which in the past equipped it well to form a stock-proof, living fence. It would grow easily, produce a natural lattice with an abundance of tightly knotted branches and spiny twigs and, unlike blackthorn, was less inclined to sucker out into pasture. It also grew and to some extent still does, as a woodland margin tree and in some instances can form a sturdy trunk. Hawthorn has many mystical connotations, and various dire tales are related of misfortune befalling those who interfered with the 'fairy tree'. A number of these isolated trees and gnarled bushes have survived, redolent of history. Many of these revered bushes have been removed from the landscape by modernising farmers without any obvious ill effects, although the ring or 'fairy' forts and other ancient archaeological features with which they were often associated seem mystically to have been spirited away.

Hedges dominated by Hawthorn are usually planted features, especially where the field boundaries have been planned and arranged in unnaturally straight lines. Hawthorn usually comes into flower in May, shortly after the leaves have flushed.

Hawthorn

Kidney Vetch

Anthyllis vulneraria

Kidney Vetch is an important element in sand-dune vegetation, occurring also on maritime grassland, on sheltered headlands and inland on gravel features. The prevailing flower colour is yellow, but it also occurs in some unusual creamy-white and reddish variations. The plant has added significance in being the preferred food-plant for the caterpillars of the Small Blue Butterfly, which form their pupal cases among the dried-out fruiting heads. Unfortunately many of its inland sites have now been destroyed — the gravel pits where it once was common are increasingly used for land-fill or as feeding areas for livestock.

Wood Sorrel

Oxalis acetosella

Wood Sorrel is one of the few flowering species that can cope with low light conditions. Its bright white petals, delicately veined with pale purple lines, flower from late spring onward, its distinct three-lobed leaves sometimes eaten as a salad (the sharp flavour comes from oxalic acid). It is usually more common in slightly shaded, acid ground conditions including hedgerow banks, but can also grow in woodlands on limestone soils, especially on the slightly more acid conditions of fallen logs where it is isolated from more lime-rich ground conditions.

Many other *Oxalis* species have been introduced into gardens in Ireland and some are now becoming established on roadsides and waste ground near gardens from where they have been ejected because of their aggressive and persistently invasive tendencies. Some species are on the way to becoming global pests and one yellow-flowered species is a regular nuisance in greenhouses in Ireland.

Wood Anemone

Anemone nemorosa

Wood Anemone forms great sheets of white flowers in woods in springtime. A member of the Buttercup family, it is also a relative of *Clematis* and the more flashy garden anemones. The flowers, which are positioned on the tips of slender stalks, nod in the wind — hence the older name of Windflower. Wood Anemone is especially typical of natural woodlands that have formed on limestone soils but has been lost from many of its former sites where cattle have been over-wintered in small woodlands.

Wood Anemone

Wood Sorrel

Summer

Water Avens

Geum rivale

Water Avens is typically found on the edges of damp deciduous woods rather than in the interior. It can also grow in the open on wet, sloping ground. It is a close relative of the more familiar Wood Avens, a plant of woodland paths, hedgerows and even older suburbs. They sometimes form interesting hybrids where the two parents come into contact.

Puffin

Fratercula arctica
Puifín

The most colourful and recognisable member of the auk family, Puffins are found on remote coastal islands and undisturbed cliffs. Unlike Razorbills and Guillemots which nest on the bare ledges of cliffs, Puffins nest in disused shearwater or Rabbit burrows and feed their chick inside the burrow for up to six weeks. The main diet of the young birds is Sandeels and Sprats which thrive in the cool seas off Ireland. However, increases in sea temperatures could threaten this vital seabird food supply. When the Puffin chick is almost fully grown, the adults abandon it and, forced by hunger, the chick eventually emerges under the cover of darkness and flies out to sea. At this stage the young bird is totally independent. In winter Puffins disperse far out into the Atlantic and are rarely seen in offshore waters. Their large, bright, colourful bills, which makes them so recognisable, lose the outer layers in winter and become duller and smaller. These birds were photographed on Great Saltee Island, Wexford.

Otter

Lutra lutra
Dobharchú/Madra uisce

With its long, muscular, streamlined body, webbed feet and flattened tail, the otter is a consummate swimmer. When an otter emerges from water it appears to be covered in short spines or scales. This is because it has long, oily guard hairs protruding through the thick underfur. These oily hairs tend to be repelled by water and stick together until the fur dries out.

When cruising by paddling at the surface, otters ride relatively low in the water and usually only the top of the head and part of the tail are visible. They arch their back when they dive and the body appears to glisten as the long guard hairs bend over and trap a layer of air that insulates the animal and keeps the underfur dry. They swim by flexing their body and tail up and down, moving their long hind legs in parallel, while keeping the shorter forelegs tucked close to the body.

Otters are rarely far from water. They are widespread in Ireland and may be found on rivers, streams, lakes, marshes, estuaries, on the coast and even within urban areas. Nevertheless, because they are quite shy, the first sign of their presence is often a pile of their droppings (spraint) deposited as a marker at strategic locations within their home range. Regularly-used sprainting sites include grassy mounds on the riverbank, large rocks beside or within the river bed, or the ledges at or under bridges. In fact, recording spraints is how an otter population is monitored. These spraints also provide information on the otter's diet since they usually contain indigestible remains of their prey. They may eat eels, salmon, trout, dace frogs, perch, roach, crayfish, wrasse, crabs and occasionally waterbirds.

Otters may breed at any time of the year but more usually in spring and summer and after about nine weeks give birth to between one and five (usually two) cubs that are weaned about 15 weeks later.

Yellow Horned-poppy

Glaucium flavum

The plant that best characterises maritime shingle ridges all around the Irish coast is Yellow Horned-poppy. It can be biennial or perennial. Surviving on coastal shingle can be a struggle. Stones on the shore are constantly moved by the waves, grinding any living plants to pulp. However, this poppy produces large numbers of seeds in the long (often 20cm), curved pods that give the plant its name. These can remain in a dormant state until the right combination of tides and winter wave action brings them to a higher place on the shore where they can germinate in relative safety. The plants form dense cushions of glaucous, hairy leaves from which the flowering stems emerge to produce short-lived, individual, large, yellow flowers.

Dunlin

Calidris alpina
Breacóg

While a common autumn and winter visitor, Dunlin is a scarce breeding species found on some inland wetlands and coastal islands in western and north-western regions of Ireland. In summer plumage, the birds change from their winter greys to show rich chestnut upperparts and a striking black belly patch. Nesting on the ground, such plumage allows the bird to remain camouflaged when incubating the eggs or brooding its young. Despite that, during the breeding season the males attract attention by engaging in courtship and territorial displays involving slow flights and calling. They will perch prominently on elevated spots within their territory and watch over their areas for possible incursions from neighbouring males. This bird was photographed on Inishbofin, Donegal.

Woody Nightshade

Solanum dulcamara

Woody Nightshade occurs naturally in the band of vegetation that fringes the banks and shores of our rivers and lakes. Here it climbs up, its woody scrambling stem lifting its flowering sprays well over the water. It starts flowering in early summer and produces bunches of juicy, red berries in autumn. It can more frequently be encountered in hedgerows, especially those with adjoining drains and has spread into this type of habitat throughout most of the countryside. Its blue petals contrast strongly with the cluster of protruding, yellow anthers — a floral structure which it shares with the potato and tomato. It is possible that in the north-west of Ireland it may be a relic of cultivation. It had many medicinal uses and had acquired a variety of vernacular names, reflecting its importance and familiarity to herbalists in earlier times.

Yellow Water-lily

Nuphar lutea

White Water-lily

Nymphaea alba

The colourful flowers of Yellow Water-lily will be familiar to most people who live near a canal. It is one of the few aquatic species that can withstand canal vegetation clearance schemes. It produces two types of leaves — the familiar firm, leathery, lily-pad types of the surface but also larger, softer, submerged leaves that can escape the blade of the weed boats. Originally (and still) a species of nutrient-rich waters of lake margins and larger rivers, it has spread along the canal systems and is sometimes now included in ornamental water planting schemes. In autumn large fruits, about the size of a small lemon, are produced and are carried above water until their supporting stems collapse.

In more base-poor waters, especially in the north and west, its counterpart, White Water-lily (over), is common, especially in bog pools, small lakes and even slow-moving rivers. Both species have been introduced into areas far beyond their natural ranges as attractive pond plants.

White Water-lily

Corncrake

Crex crex
Traonach

Once a very common summer visitor and widespread breeding species, Corncrakes are now globally endangered. Found in hay meadows and grasslands, the birds are more often heard than seen, their rasping *kerrx-kerrx* call being a once familiar sound of the Irish countryside. Changes in farming practices such as the early cutting of the grasslands meant the birds had fewer opportunities to breed and, coupled with pressures of hunting of the birds on migration and habitat loss in their wintering grounds in southern Africa, the Corncrake population has declined drastically over the past 30 years. Conservation measures in Ireland included the management of large areas of grass meadows along the Shannon in the midlands but successive wet summers forced the birds to abandon those areas. Corncrakes are now present in summer in small numbers on islands in the north-west, west and some areas of the south-west. This bird was photographed on Inishbofin, Donegal.

Soprano Pipistrelle

Pipistrellus pygmaeus
Ialtóg fheascrach sopránach

About twenty years ago Ireland's biologists believed that we had only one pipistrelle, the Common Pipistrelle. In fact biologists worldwide were completely unaware of the existence of the Soprano Pipistrelle. Then gradually it became apparent that Common Pipistrelles were using two different ultrasound frequencies to catch their prey. These were referred to as phonic types. Further observations indicated that all members of a colony of pipistrelles used one or other of these frequencies. This now raised the possibility that the Common Pipistrelle might consist of two species that were so far impossible to tell apart. The bats, however, had no such difficulties and when it was shown that bats would only breed with individuals of the same phonic type, it was clear that we were dealing with two species that were almost identical. Further genetic research confirmed in 1997 that this was so. And just like the emperor's new clothes, as soon as the existence of the Soprano Pipistrelle was confirmed, subtle differences between it and the Common Pipistrelle began to be noticed. The face is darker than that of the Common Pipistrelle and it is slightly smaller. This is Ireland's smallest bat and never weighs more than 8g. It has longish, narrow wings typical of a fast flier but it is also fairly manoeuvrable and it flies usually about 2–3 metres above the ground. It emerges to hunt just after dusk, although its most usual prey — midges — are most active just before dusk.

The Soprano Pipistrelle can be found in urban and rural areas and often flies around streetlights or along linear features of the habitat such as hedges, treelines or waterside vegetation. Its feeding sites are usually not far from water and it appears to forage farther from its roost than does the Common Pipistrelle. It catches smaller prey than the Common Pipistrelle, mainly midges, mosquitoes and small caddis flies. When feeding most ravenously, it can catch 15 insects per minute and over 3,000 in one night.

The Soprano Pipistrelle tends to have its summer roosts in confined spaces in old and new buildings. The location seems to be more important than the precise structure of the building. It chooses cavities and recesses, such as the space behind window-sashes, under weather boards, behind fascia boards, within the structure of flat roofs and in cavity walls.

Water Mint

Mentha aquatica

The scent of Water Mint is often detected long before the plant is encountered. The stems bear a single cluster of individual, small, bluish-lilac flowers arranged at the top of the stem and the scent comes from the leaves. Water Mint is widespread throughout Ireland in a wide variety of wet-ground habitats. A second species, Corn Mint, *Mentha arvensis*, was once much more widespread but is now found mainly on slightly damp, neutral to acid arable soils especially in drumlin country. Corn Mint is a late-summer flowerer, bearing several clusters of flowers arranged in clumps along the flowering stem at the leaf bases. It has a heavier, minty smell. These two species occasionally hybridise and the resulting progeny grows vigorously, sometimes in the absence of one or even both parents. Indeed there are many hybrids within the mint family, originating as culinary herbs, and a number of these have found their way onto roadsides and river banks where they have spread widely.

Gannet

Morus bassanus
Gainéad

Our largest seabird with a wingspan of almost two metres, Gannets are found at colonies in Dublin, Wexford and Cork, with the largest being on the Little Skellig, Kerry, where over 20,000 pairs nest each summer. Building nests made of seaweed and other marine debris such as old fishing nets, Gannets repair and add to their nests each year. They are long-lived birds and pair for life but raise just one chick each year. With binocular vision and specially reinforced skulls, the birds are highly evolved for fishing at sea. Diving from heights of 40 metres or more, they sweep their wings back over their bodies and enter the water at great speeds. Their long wings also allow them to glide and fly effortlessly over the stormiest of seas, and during the breeding season adults can fly several hundreds of kilometres each day in search of food for their chicks. In winter many adults will move south off Europe but others stay close to the breeding sites. Young birds tend to move further south and can winter off West Africa. This image of a Gannet in flight was captured at sea off Kerry.

Foxglove

Digitalis purpurea

Foxglove (or Lady's fingers) is widespread on dry, acid soils and is a good indicator of the point on a roadside or hedge bank on low, hilly ground where the lime-rich, glacial-drift soils peter out and the underlying acid rocks protrude. Various colour forms can be persuaded to grow on limy soils but there are other species in cultivation that seem to tolerate these conditions with greater ease. Foxglove was widely esteemed as a herbal cure for many ailments in the past, but it was only following the researches of Withering (c. 1785) that its clinical virtues in relation to heart failure were fully appreciated. Withering's investigations, particularly in relation to dosage levels, led to his widespread recognition as a pioneer pharmacologist.

Brown Hare

Lepus europaeus
Giorria gallda

If you should see hares cavorting about the fields of County Tyrone or County Derry in mid-Ulster in spring or early summer, there is a 50:50 chance that they might be Brown Hares. This is another of our recent introductions. Brown Hares are not native to Ireland but have been introduced several times to a number of locations during the second half of the 19th and the early part of the 20th century. The only populations to become established were in mid-Ulster. On a global scale the Brown Hare is the southern counterpart of the Mountain Hare and is found, from Britain and Western Europe, as far east as central Asia. The Brown Hare is larger than the Mountain Hare. Its ears are relatively longer and if folded downwards would reach the tip of its nose. Its coat is yellowish brown and sometimes mottled in summer, which has given it its local name of 'Thrush Hare'. Its winter coat is reddish and it never grows a white winter coat.

Ecologically it is a creature of more benign climates and habitats and is typical of lowland areas with arable crops and open grassland. It feeds on herbs, grasses, young cereal crops, young root crops and buds and leaves of shrubs. Brown Hares are reported to be quite excitable and difficult to maintain in captivity — a factor that may have spared them from being used for coursing. They rest and nest in the open and rely on their mottled coat for camouflage and on their speed and stamina to evade pursuing predators.

Brown Hares have up to now not proved particularly invasive in Ireland. All but one or two of about fourteen introductions have failed to produce viable populations. But the established population poses a potential threat to the native Irish Hare. Their diets are almost identical so they are in direct competition and a small change in land use towards more arable agriculture might tip the balance entirely in favour of the Brown Hare. Furthermore, there is also a threat of hybridisation between the two species which if it was progressive would destroy the genetic integrity of the Irish Hare. Indeed interbreeding may be more than a mere threat since a number of individuals of intermediate appearance have been reported, but their true nature has not yet been established.

Guillemot

Uria aalge
Foracha

A common breeding seabird found in large, noisy colonies on steep cliffs around our coastlines and islands, Guillemots are a member of the auk family. The birds do not build a nest but lay a single egg on the bare rocks of the cliff ledge. Guillemot eggs are very pointed at one end so that, should the birds touch off the egg when leaving the cliffs, the egg will roll in on itself. When the chick hatches, it is fed by both parents with partially digested fish. However, as the bird gets older, the demand for food increases and this creates a serious problem for the parents. If they leave the chick alone and go in search of food, it will be an easy target for hungry gulls. So, when a chick is only two weeks old, an adult bird (usually the male) will lead it to the edge of the cliff and encourage it to jump into the sea below. These little chicks cannot fly but use their tiny wings and outstretched feet to slow their descent. Once on the water, the adult leads them out to sea. The young bird will spend several weeks being fed at sea by the adults before being fully fledged and independent. This Guillemot and chick was photographed on Great Saltee Island, Wexford.

Grey Wagtail

Motacilla cinerea
Glasóg liath

Grey Wagtails are colourful and active birds that hunt for insects, larvae and caterpillars among the vegetation of river banks. They will also catch flies on the wing. Like all insect-eaters, their long, thin, pointed bill is ideally suited to snatching prey from the air or picking it delicately from leaves and plants. This bird had captured a tiny caterpillar and held it for several minutes at the tip of its beak before flying off to feed his hungry brood of chicks. Both sexes are colourful but the male is brighter and shows more extensive black on the chin. This male was one of a pair nesting along the River Dodder, Dublin.

Montbretia

Crocosmia x crocosmiiflora

Montbretia, a hybrid of garden origin between two South African species, is so widely established in Ireland that it is sometimes mistaken for a native plant. It is particularly abundant on roadsides in western Ireland where it forms dense stands. It can do this because the plants have corms but then produce rhizomes which spread and coalesce. It is now taking hold in other parts of Ireland and is particularly destructive in natural habitats where it physically ousts the less assertive, less robust indigenous flora.

Badger

Meles meles
Broc

The badger is one of our most widespread mammals and there are at least a quarter of a million badgers in Ireland. Because of its nocturnal lifestyle and foraging behaviour it is also probably more often seen dead than alive. There can scarcely be anyone in the country who has not seen the carcase of a badger, a victim of a road traffic impact. The numbers who have seen a live badger are substantially fewer but there is probably no animal that is so rewarding for any effort invested in observing it. It is the most dumpy of the Irish members of the family *Mustelidae*, such as stoats, otters and Pine Martens. Ireland is at the western edge of its range, which extends eastward as far as Japan. It is typically a creature of woodland but in Ireland it has adapted well to a relatively deforested landscape. Most of its setts are constructed in hedgerows separating agricultural fields. The setts are a system of underground tunnels, sometimes up to 100 metres long and entrances, occasionally over 20, that contain a number of living chambers. Setts are important to badgers and may be occupied continuously for hundreds of years. For this reason they are protected by law. Badgers appear to be obsessive diggers and spend considerable time and energy maintaining, extending and modifying their setts. An opening with signs of fresh digging and piles of discarded bedding nearby in the spring is usually a reliable indication of an occupied sett and probably the presence of a breeding female. Badgers are extremely territorial and they mark the boundaries of the family territory at key latrine sites at which they deposit faeces and a sticky secretion from under the tail.

Badgers do not hibernate but tend to spend more time underground during mid-winter. There are usually two periods, spring and autumn, when road casualties are more common. Spring casualties tend to be dominated by young males leaving their families, dispersing to strike out on their own, and by adults in breeding condition seeking partners; autumn casualties tend to be breeding adults. Adult badgers mate either in late spring (April–May) or in autumn (yearling females), but gestation proper does not begin until late December. As a result cubs are born mostly in February and March.

Badgers will eat almost anything. Although they are social, they usually forage alone. In Ireland most of their foraging is along hedgerows and in arable and pasture fields. They eat earthworms, beetles, slugs, snails, leatherjackets, cockchafers, insect larvae, frogs, frogspawn, rats, young rabbits, mice, hedgehogs, cereals, apples, elderberries, fungi and clover. Despite this variety, hot, dry summers and cold winters are often difficult times for badgers. Badgers find peanuts very acceptable and they will soon learn to regularly visit a site at which peanuts are scattered.

Badgers are creatures of habit and use the same paths around their territory. These paths have often been in use for decades by several generations of badgers. This explains why there are many accident black-spots for road accidents involving badgers.

Thrift

Thrift

Armeria maritima

Thrift (pages 102–3) is predominantly a plant of sea-cliffs and salt-marshes where it can form dense cushions or solid mats of vegetation. On cliffs it produces tough roots that work their way through the soil, often holding it together, the dense leaves resisting the impact of the waves in the spray zone. Conditions are less physically stressful in the salt marshes and here Thrift can form a virtual monoculture. It can also do this on sea-sprayed earthen cliffs up to the point where the farmed landscape begins. Unusually, Thrift can grow on some mountains where it has the appearance of a smart, compact alpine. Although it does not need salt, it can clearly do far better when it has some.

Oak canopy

As summer approaches the leaf canopy begins to close in. Less light falls on the ground and the spring flora disappears. Seeds fall to the ground to remain dormant until the following spring. Many non-woody perennial species die back and by late summer there is no trace above ground of many of the more common species.

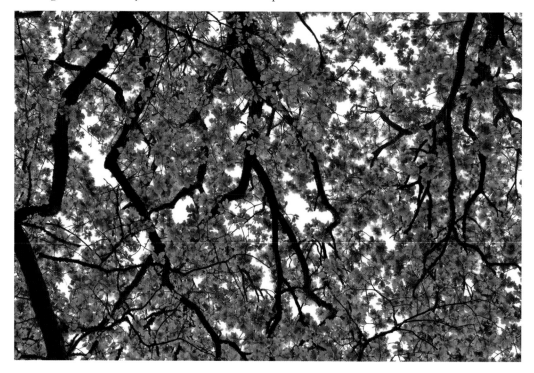

Blue Tit

Cyanistes caeruleus
Meantán gorm

One of Ireland's commonest and most recognisable bird species, Blue Tits are found in a wide variety of habitats, from woodlands and hedgerows to parks and gardens. They nest in holes in trees and walls and will also readily take to nestboxes. Unlike other small birds, they will raise just one family in a season, laying as many as eight eggs. It is estimated that during the three-week period that the young are in the nest, they will require as many as 18,000 food items such as flies, small spiders, caterpillars and other insect larvae. Blue Tits time their nesting to coincide with the greatest availability of such prey, but during some summers long periods of heavy rain result in many nests failing to raise any young at all. This bird, photographed in Cork during heavy rain, was nesting a little later than normal and the pair successfully raised five young.

Rabbit

Oryctolagus cuniculus
Coinín

The Rabbit is one of the Norman invaders, introduced during the 12th century, into enclosures termed coney-garths, and bred for the table and for their fur. But their legendary fertility is matched only by their powers of escape and they soon absconded and became established throughout the country. So great was their impact on the landscape that many placenames in Ireland refer to Rabbits.

Rabbits are grazers and they thrive on short grass pastures which they maintain by their almost constant feeding. They are mainly nocturnal, particularly if they are subjected to regular hunting. But in spring and summer thay may be quite active at dawn and dusk and there can be scarcely a more endearing sight, on a summer evening, than that of a colony of Rabbits busily grazing on a west-facing grassy bank, interrupted now and then by playful chases and episodes of digging.

Rabbits superficially resemble scaled-down hares but the resemblance ends there. While hares relish the open and rely on speed and stamina, Rabbits have taken a different track. Unlike hares, they live in burrow systems called warrens, and if the colony is large it may be subdivided into a number of clans, with strict hierarchies keeping order. In addition, Rabbits — uneasy in the open — are rarely found far from their warren. When danger threatens, a warning squeal or thumping spreads through the group and they dash to the safety of the warren. By their very nature Rabbits are sprinters and cannot maintain high speed for very long. This ties them to the vicinity of their warrens but has saved them from the persecution of coursing.

Rabbits may breed through most of the year but usually between February and September, depending on weather, food supply and population density. Females only ovulate after they mate, and courting Rabbits are amorous and aggressive in almost equal measure. Courtship is confusing to watch because often several males are squabbling over a breeding female who often herself seems hostile to them all. All of this is expressed in hectic chases, biting, kicking and boxing. Nevertheless, females may breed between three and seven times a year and produce between three and seven kittens each time. Indeed females born early in the year may themselves breed before the following winter.

(Eric Dempsey)

Common Cow-wheat

Melampyrum pratense

One of the few colourful species to thrive in natural acid woodland in summer is Common Cow-wheat. The bright yellow, drooping flowers contrast with the dark blue centre, a feature not immediately evident unless the flower tube is examined at close range. It can also grow in heathy ground and even on dried-out raised bogs and can sometimes be found where pines have been interplanted among oak trees in rocky ground.

Louseworts

Pedicularis palustris, Pedicularis sylvatica

To judge from the botanical records made more than a century ago our two species of Lousewort, Marsh Lousewort, *Pedicularis palustris*, and Lousewort proper, *P. sylvatica*, were more or less equally common. The former is a plant of fenny ground and marshes while the latter is more usually encountered in damp ground in slightly acid conditions such as moorland. By now, many of the sites for Marsh Lousewort have been lost. It is a shallowly-rooting species, at its best in thinly vegetated, muddy ground. As soil water levels drop this species dies out rapidly, especially if followed up by grazing. In contrast, Lousewort has held its own in many upland, agriculturally-marginal areas.

Harebell

Campanula rotundifolia

Harebell is an abundant plant of free-draining ground, shallow soils over rock, sand-dunes and even uplands. It is particularly abundant in the Burren but occurs also on sea cliffs around most of our coast. In many ways it characterises the natural, undamaged, open-ground wilderness, surviving where grazing levels are slight but at levels sufficient to inhibit scrub invasion. It begins to flower towards the end of summer. Prior to that it is not a conspicuous plant.

Common Twayblade

Neottia ovata

Common Twayblade is an orchid which has two large basal leaves (hence the name) and is particularly successful in dune slacks, damp fenny grassland and fenny bog margins where grazing is slight but scrub has not encroached. It usually occurs in areas where many other interesting species are also present. Higher levels of grazing will inhibit scrub invasion or re-invasion and cattle will cut up or poach the soft, wet ground. Finding the best grazing levels to protect and maintain biodiversity is not easy in conditions where the sustainable carrying capacity of a site can be distorted by the availability of price supports. A second species, Lesser Twayblade, *Neottia cordata*, occurs in small numbers under heather in upland areas. For many years the Twayblades were included in the genus *Listera* but recent molecular research has required that they be transferred to the genus *Neottia*, which includes the rare Bird's-nest Orchid, *N. nidus-avis*, a saprophytic species of orchid, lacking chlorophyll, from shaded woods.

Jay

Garrulus glandarius
Scréachóg

One of Ireland's most colourful members of the crow family, Jays are found in woodlands in all regions of the country. However, they are usually extremely shy and their raucous calls are often the only indicator of their presence. In autumn they collect and store food such as acorns and are noted for their ability to remember the exact locations of their food stashes, even digging in snow in winter to retrieve food. However, in some areas, birds become accustomed to people and can be more confiding in their behaviour. This individual was photographed in the Phoenix Park, Dublin. The bird was taking advantage of an abundance of food left for the ducks near one of the ponds and visited the site on a regular basis. On this occasion it was rewarded with a large piece of digestive biscuit. Ireland has a unique race of Jay which differs from British and European birds by appearing darker and showing more extensive, broader streaking on the crown.

Rosebay Willowherb

Chamerion angustifolium

Rosebay Willowherb was once a rare species of mountain scree slopes. In Britain it became widely established after the Second World War on bombed sites, gaining the popular name Fireweed. In Ireland, through the 20th century the species began to spread onto bog margins, railway lines, urban wastelands and builders' rubble in so-called areas of urban renewal, especially when the process of renewal became stalled. In recent times it has also become a spectacular feature of recently-felled woodlands where it can form dense perennial stands aided by its rhizomatous growth form. It produces thousands of tiny, parachute-borne seeds and can become a dangerously invasive species in a very short time.

Humpback Whale

Megaptera novaeangliae
Míol mór dronnach

Although they are widespread throughout the world's oceans, Humpback Whales occasionally, and thankfully more frequently of late, present one of our most awe-inspiring wildlife spectacles. To witness such an enormous and majestic creature launch its 40-tonne body out of the ocean, executing a backward flip before crashing back with a tremendous splash, is a rare privilege. This is the quintessential whale, large (about the eighth largest living whale), inquisitive, active and extremely vocal. There can be hardly a person with an interest in wildlife who has not heard a recording of the song of the Humpback Whale. Indeed a famous traditional tune, 'Port na bPúcaí', from the Blasket Islands, is almost certainly a rendering of the song of the Humpback Whale. Humpback Whales were once hunted from Ireland in the early 20th century, and were almost hunted to extinction worldwide. Now they are recovering and are being sighted more frequently off the south and west coasts. The Humpback Whales of the eastern Atlantic spend the winter in northern waters off Iceland and Scandinavia where they gorge on small shoaling fish and crustaceans. They are extremely resourceful hunters and have a number of ingenious tactics to catch different kinds of prey. They migrate along the west coast of Ireland on their journey between their feeding grounds and their breeding grounds in the south, probably near the Cape Verde Islands off North West Africa. They probably give birth in spring, mating takes place soon afterwards and they then begin their northward journey to the feeding grounds.

Corn Poppy

Corn Poppy

Papaver rhoeas

The widespread Corn Poppy (pages 118–19) produces thousands of seeds from a single plant. These are contained in little capsules, each with a ring of holes at the top, out of which the seeds are scattered as the stems sway in the wind. The capsules have been likened to old-fashioned pepper-canisters. The seeds do not all germinate in the following spring and tend to move downwards in the soil profile, carried by rainwater and underground soil movements where they remain dormant in colder and darker conditions. Many remain viable in the soil and will germinate in subsequent years when the soil is disturbed by ploughing, digging the foundations for houses and motorway construction. The seeds are raised to a warmer place and there germinate in their thousands. The floral memorial emblem of the First World War was well chosen.

Poppies were once widespread in cornfields but are very sensitive to herbicide. However, they still put in an appearance after ploughing, especially on field margins or where spraying has not been successful. There are various species of red-flowered poppy in Ireland. Corn Poppy has a smooth, round fruit. A second species, Long-headed Poppy, *P. dubium*, has an elongate but also smooth capsule. Other poppies with spiny fruits formerly found on sandy ground near the sea are much rarer nowadays. The Opium Poppy, *P. somniferum*, with large, pinkish flowers and glaucous, clasping stem leaves is a garden relic which often turns up around municipal refuse tips and waste ground.

Hairy Bindweed

Calystegia pulchrum

Although we have a number of native bindweeds, the most conspicuous species by now are those that have been introduced. This large pink one, Hairy Bindweed, is becoming an increasing feature of the landscape, climbing up into hedgerows in many parts of Ireland. Another species with similarly large flowers, usually white and sometimes with pale-pink striping, Large Bindweed, *C. sylvatica*, is well established by now throughout towns and cities, flowering there well into late autumn. Our native species, Hedge Bindweed, *C. sepium*, is a smaller-flowered plant, uniformly white usually, and most common in slightly more natural habitats such as river systems and scrubby bog margins where grazing is slight. A fourth, much smaller species, Sea Bindweed, *C. soldanella*, is scattered around the coast. This native species grows on loose sand in outer dune systems, either among the Marram grass or further out on the foreshore, especially where the terrain has been stiffened by shingle. Its stems grow through the sand, pushing up kidney-shaped leaves and large, pink flowers, striped white.

Eyebrights

Euphrasia

Eyebrights of the genus *Euphrasia* are often encountered in a variety of brightly-lit natural habitats, ranging from thinly vegetated fen peat to lime-rich grasslands, sand-dunes and base-poor moorland margins. Their presence is indicative of a degree of naturalness of habitat, and they are intolerant of heavy grazing and are poorly equipped to cope in silage grasslands. In the past they were widely employed by herbalists as a cure for disorders of the eye. Eyebrights are not easy to identify to species level owing to their propensity to hybridise and to form intermediate populations. There is one highly distinctive species, however, which is very common in parts of western Ireland and elsewhere on shallow, rocky and sandy ground near the sea. This is the so-called Irish Eyebright, *Euphrasia salisburgensis*, which as its name suggests is known from central Europe, but the plants from Ireland are considered to be sufficiently different to have been given the varietal name var. *hibernica*.

Swift

Apus apus
Gabhlán gaoithe

True masters of the air, Swifts are among the fastest flying birds in the world. They are so highly evolved for flight, they have lost the ability to walk and, when they return from their wintering grounds in South Africa, nest in cavities in old buildings. In order to climb into the nest, they crawl, bat-like, up the side of the building before going into the nest. On the wing, the birds catch all the food they need and even get enough liquid from the insects they eat. As well as eating while flying, Swifts are among the few species in the world that mate and even sleep on the wing. A pair can raise up to three young in a brood and feeds them on insects that are collected on the wing and stored in a pouch in the throat. This image of an adult with a full pouch of insects was captured in Swords, Dublin. When the young are fully grown, the parents stop visiting them and, forced by hunger, the young birds leave the safety of the nest and take flight for the first time. They are then totally independent and must fend for themselves immediately. Like the adults, young birds migrate to South Africa and will not return to Ireland until they are two or three years old. Research has shown that from the time a young Swift leaves the nest until it returns to breed for the first time perhaps three years later, it may have spent that entire period flying non-stop.

Dipper

Cinclus cinclus
Gabha dubh

A bird of fast-flowing rivers, Dippers dive under the water to hunt for insect and fish larvae among the stones of riverbeds. They will also walk, head under the water, along the shallow sections of rivers in search of food. They usually perch openly on favourite rocks along rivers. When perched, they constantly bob up and down, and the white membrane (the nictitating membrane), which protects the eyes when under the water, is very obvious when the birds blink. More normally associated with upland rivers, birds can be found at all altitudes and can occur close to cities and towns. They build nests under bridges but, on occasions, can nest under waterfalls and weirs. Ireland has a unique race of Dipper which shows a narrow, bright chestnut band on the breast just below the white breast gorget. This adult was feeding two young along a river in Dublin.

Butterfly Orchids

Platanthera bifolia, Platanthera chlorantha

Orchids of any type are vital indicators of good habitat conditions. They occupy a wide range of natural habitats, and the presence of any individual species usually implies that there has been a continuity of favourable environmental conditions. Butterfly Orchids are good examples. We have two species, Lesser Butterfly Orchid, *Platanthera bifolia*, and Greater Butterfly Orchid, *P. chlorantha*. The former occurs especially in the lowlands on the edges of bogs and fens while in Ireland Greater Butterfly Orchid is more common on higher ground, typically on slightly damp, grassy slopes where the ground begins to become heathy.

Chough

Pyrrhocorax pyrrhocorax
Cág cosdearg

A very beautiful member of the crow family, Choughs are best recognised by their bright red bills and legs. Found along the coast in southern, western and northern regions, they are true masters of the air and can be seen in family groups flying effortlessly over seacliffs, giving their loud *chouu* calls from which the species derives its name. They feed along areas of coastal sand-dunes and short grasslands and take a variety of insects and larvae, using their long bills to dig up their prey. Nesting in crevices and caves on coastal cliffs as well as in old buildings, they can have as many as four chicks in a season. This group image was taken on Great Saltee Island, Wexford, and shows two adults with one of two young they successfully raised. The young bird is in the middle and is recognised by its paler bill and legs.

Sand Martin

Riparia riparia
Gabhlán gainimh

One of the first migrants to return to Ireland from their sub-Saharan wintering grounds in spring, Sand Martins are a common breeding species. Nesting in colonies, they excavate tunnels in open sand cliffs, quarries and even cut-away bogs. They line the chamber at the end of the tunnel with grasses and feathers and can raise two families in a season. Catching insects on the wing, the adults return to feed their young inside the chamber. As the young grow older, they venture further out of the tunnel until, about ready to fledge, they view the comings and goings of the colony from the tunnel entrance. These young birds were waiting patiently for an adult to return and begged with great enthusiasm when the parent arrived with food. This image was captured at an old building site, close to a busy main road in Antrim.

Sea-spurreys

Spergularia

Sea-spurreys occur at different points along the shore, at levels related to tidal inundation and exposure. All three coastal species produce pink flowers and are conspicuous elements of the coastal flora from early summer onwards. Rock Sea-spurrey, *S. rupicola*, can be almost woody at the base and anchors itself by the roots in crevices in sea-sprayed rocks and harbour walls. A similarly large species, Greater Sea-spurrey, *S. media*, occurs mainly in salt marshes. A third species, Lesser Sea-spurrey, *S. marina*, has smaller petals which can sometimes be almost white. It can grow well far from the open sea, colonising estuaries but also spreading further inland along the banks of drainage ditches and even growing on muddy saline patches as a fast-growing annual. A much rarer species, Sand Spurrey, *S. rubra*, is not a coastal plant, living instead on sandy, acid gravels in upland areas especially on the sides of forestry tracks.

Kestrel

Falco tinnunculus
Pocaire gaoithe

One of our most common birds of prey, Kestrels show the pointed wingtips typical of falcons. However, unlike other species of falcon such as Peregrine and Merlin which engage in fast pursuits of their prey, Kestrels hunt by hovering motionless, head into the wind, using the wings and tail to make minor adjustments as they hang in the air. They feed on a variety of small birds and rodents but will also take insects and worms. When hovering, the birds are not just looking for movements but are also tracking the scent trails of rodents that mark their territory with urine. Kestrels see the world in ultraviolet and such scent marks glow when seen in that spectrum. Nesting on cliffs ledges, old buildings and occasionally holes in trees, a pair can raise as many as five chicks. All birds of prey adopt asynchronous-hatching which means that, as each egg is laid, the female will commence incubation. This results in each chick hatching at least two days ahead of the next so that in a family of five, the oldest can be as much as ten days older than the youngest. In summers when there is a plentiful food supply, all the chicks will survive, but if food is short, only the oldest will fledge. All five chicks from this nest, photographed in Dublin, were well fed and all fledged successfully. Males are more colourful than females and this hunting adult male was also photographed in Dublin.

Knapweed

Centaurea nigra
Centaurea scabiosa

Common Knapweed, *Centaurea nigra*, is one of our most widespread perennial herbs, especially on dry roadside verges, banks and undamaged, semi-natural grassland; and it is even able to hold its own in rough pasture despite having an erect, narrow shape that renders it vulnerable to grazing and mowing. It has a long flowering season and brightens many roadsides throughout the island. More importantly, it often points to sites where smaller and sometimes rarer species of lime-rich grasslands find refuge.

A larger species, Greater Knapweed, *Centaurea scabiosa*, should be looked out for. Not only is it taller and generally more robust, but the outer flowers are distinctly longer than the inner ones. This species is much rarer but is common on roadsides especially in the Burren and on earth-covered sea cliffs and also turns up occasionally but persistently on railway embankments, safe from grazing though not from herbicide application.

A third species, Cornflower, *Centaurea cyanus*, was once an established cornfield weed associated with particular types of cereal cultivation. It still turns up occasionally where land in these areas has been turned over. However, it is now included in wild flower seed mixtures, with the result that most of the plants encountered on motorway verges and in other amenity plantings have been introduced to areas where they may never have occurred.

Greater Knapweed

Common Knapweed

Natterjack Toad

Epidalea calamita
Cnádán

This is one of Ireland's most scarce, restricted and enigmatic amphibians. It is our only toad and for many years it was a mystery how it got here. This is because it is confined to a few locations on the Iveragh and Dingle peninsulas in County Kerry and to a population deliberately established at the Raven Nature Reserve in County Wexford. It is a member of an unusual group of species united only because they are found in Spain and Portugal on the one hand and Ireland on the other and not in between. The usual explanations for this were that the Natterjack arrived naturally overland from Iberia after the end of the last ice age, or was transported from there by early or quite recent human colonists. Alternatively, Natterjacks may have been widespread before the ice age and survived in a refuge somewhere in or near the south-west of Ireland. Recent genetic evidence indicates that the latter is most likely to be the true explanation. Therefore the Natterjack now joins the small band of vertebrate that colonised Ireland by its own efforts. Although the Natterjack, an ectotherm, is unable to generate heat to control its temperature, it has nevertheless proven itself to have been quite durable and survived the last ice age. It presumably did so by hibernation in burrows, a habit that persists to this day. Hibernation burrows are dug in sandy soils or else the toads use spaces under stones, logs or other such niches. They become active in about April but are generally nocturnal. Natterjacks can be distinguished from frogs by virtue of their obviously drier skin and the fact that they crawl rather than hop and they have a distinctive yellow stripe down the midline of the back. They breed in April and May in shallow ponds and lay their spawn in long strings containing thousands of eggs that resemble a string of beads. The tadpoles hatch after 10 to 15 days and feed on algae or carrion in the pond. In about five to eight weeks they metamorphose into toadlets and leave the pond for up to three years before they return to breed.

Tree-mallow

Malva arborea

Tree-mallow has an unusual history in Ireland. While we are now very conscious of the impact of invasive species on the natural environment we may overlook the fact that some apparently native species can also become invasive. Tree-mallow is a large plant, unlikely to be overlooked by botanists of the 19th century and earlier. However, there are very few records from that time. Those that exist indicate a plant that occurred in very natural habitats — primarily sea cliffs and sea stacks. It is still abundant and almost dominant on some isolated sea stacks and small islands. It is much more common on the mainland nowadays, often growing on coastal shingle and in waste ground in seaside villages and even in a few places farther inland. It seems that seeds or plants were brought into cultivation from wild colonies, and subsequently spread from cottage gardens onto semi-wild or neglected patches in built-up areas. The Tree-mallow is related to the garden Hollyhocks.

Long-eared Owl

Asio otus
Ceann cait

The Long-eared Owl is the most widespread breeding owl species in Ireland and is found in woodlands where it nests in old squirrel dreys or old crow nests. During the breeding season the males proclaim their territory by giving low, muffled *oo-oo* calls. Long-eared Owls hunt by quartering over fields on silent wings or by adopting a patient sit-and-wait tactic. They will take prey ranging from rodents to small birds and even insects. Like other owl species, they cough up food pellets which consist of bone, fur and feathers — material too dangerous to pass through their digestive tracts. These pellets tell a lot about their diet, but such pellets are hard to find as the birds tend to deposit them in woodlands (finding them on the floor of an old castle is a much easier task in the case of Barn Owls). Long-eared Owls are truly nocturnal, rarely venturing out before dark. When the young leave the nest, they disperse to different areas of the woodland and begin to give very loud, squeaking, contact calls, often referred to as sounding like the 'creaking of a rusty gate'. This allows the parents to find the young and feed them. This young owlet was the youngest of five and was photographed in Dublin.

Burnet Rose

Rosa spinosissima

Burnet Rose forms a low-growing shrub and is still a common feature of many sandhill and limestone, shallow-soil habitats. Unlike most other wild roses in Ireland it does not grow well in hedges — it is not tall enough and requires open, sunny ground. It has creamy-coloured flowers and dark, almost blackish hips. Its twigs are densely covered with short prickles. This is of considerable benefit to other species of undamaged grassland systems where grazing is inhibited by the stem armature. As a result, many grazing-intolerant species were able to grow in the protection of this species. In recent years Burnet Rose has been lost from many of its former sites, especially gravel ridges. However, it still lingers on roadside verges in rocky areas and is still a strong feature of some limestone exposures. When this and other scrub-forming species such as Furze are locally eliminated, we also lose the many other species that once found here some degree of shelter from cattle and sheep.

Greater Bird's-foot Trefoil

Lotus pedunculatus

Tufted Vetch

Vicia cracca

In high summer, especially on lakeshores in drumlin country, Greater Bird's-foot Trefoil and Tufted Vetch form a distinct, coloured band defining the upper levels of the fluctuating lake levels especially in areas where grazing is light. Both species can also occur separately or in combination on the margins of boggy ground where their scrambling habit enables them to climb over other vegetation. On roadside verges both species can scramble up on lower-growing plants, flourishing until the grass is cut towards the end of summer.

Black Rat

Rattus rattus
Francach dubh

This was once one of our most common and widespread mammals. Now it is probably our rarest and not the least lamented for all that. It is probably the most destructive and dangerous mammal of all, apart from humans. It was so common on ships that it was also known as the 'ship rat'. The Black Rat in its original range is largely tree-living, a fact that made it ideally suited to exploit buildings and ships. It had arrived with early humans and was well established in Ireland by early Christian times. It then seems to have become scarce and not reappeared until medieval times. At intervals thereafter it spread terror throughout Europe as an element in the transmission of bubonic plague or black death caused by a *Yersinia* bacterium that was spread by the fleas that lived on the Black Rat. The war between humans and the Black Rat began to swing in favour of humans, in parts of Europe at least, by the arrival of the Brown Rat and the improvement in pesticides. Thousands of rats were killed annually on ships or in Dublin port alone during the 1930s, but now they are rarely found.

<-

Lakes and wetlands (page 146) receive much of their waters from rivers, streams, rivulets and small trickles. These less obvious water features, working their way through the soil, peat, rocks and vegetation, transport nutrients at a slower rate and deposit them when flow rates are slow either because of low rainfall or very gentle, sloping terrain. Nutrients therefore accumulate and concentrate in certain areas, and over time the water courses themselves block up with heavier vegetation. One of the main agents in this process is Yellow Iris, Flaggers, *Iris pseudacorus*. It has a dense, knobbly, rhizomatous rooting system and can resist sudden, water-driven erosion. It is particularly common in the flood plains of larger rivers, defining the extent of land liable to sporadic inundation, a useful quality sometimes lost on those who once would have wished to build houses or even small suburbs in such areas. There are many *Iris* species growing successfully in Irish gardens, usually in a variety of shades of blue with various yellow markings towards the centre.

->

The interface between the open sea and dry land can be very narrow, defined by little more than a band of partly overgrown, lichen-covered shoreline boulders (pages 148–9). In landscapes where there is little scope for intensive agriculture a form of semi-natural coastal and maritime grassland survives and flourishes, occasionally lightly grazed but maintained naturally by wind and sea spray. In these habitats natural processes are more visible — percolating waters work their way through the sloping soils and trickle onto the rocky shore, their pathways evidenced by the taller reedy and rushy vegetation that tracks their course.

Marsh Helleborine

Epipactis palustris

Marsh Helleborine is possibly the most distinctive of the Irish orchids. It is a species found in fens, lime-rich marshes and dune slacks and also occurs on the margins of lakeshores especially where ground water percolates over lime-rich shores. Marsh Helleborine, as well as being a conspicuous and attractive plant, has one other distinct and useful quality — it points to the potential presence of other rare and interesting species.

Grasses

Grasses, introduced or now native, or both, occupy much of the open ground of Ireland. Many of our native species are relatively small with varying degrees of value as forage. However, agronomists have bred many forms of native grasses, selected for their value as fodder, and these comprise the main bulk of the grasslands of Ireland. There is little growing space within these grasslands for the native flora even if it could gain a roothold. Most of these agricultural grasses are harvested just before they 'head up' and are converted into silage for winter feed for cattle. Some grasses are allowed grow on into summer to be cut as hay. When mature, they produce flower heads with many separate anthers where windborne pollen is produced in great quantities, much to the discomfort of asthmatics. In undamaged, natural grassland systems, many species of grass, usually smaller than the agricultural species, flourish on shallow soils over lime-rich or acid bedrock, in nutrient-poor sand-dune systems and in saline areas where their more nutrient-hungry counterparts cannot establish deep rooting systems.

Bell Heather

Erica cinerea

From late summer onwards, heathland on higher ground begins to become colourful. Two widespread, low-growing shrubs, the pink-flowered Heather, *Calluna vulgaris*, with petals united towards the base and the larger tubular purple flowers of Bell Heather, *Erica cinerea*, dominate dry, acid ground. The former is also abundant on drying-out raised bogs, often forming dense, single-species stands. Both species occur on dry heathland, a formation that is particularly widespread in Ireland and which, in combination with our native species of Furze, gives so many of our uplands their distinctive purple and gold colour. Heathlands and dry moorlands are very susceptible to burning, some of which occurs accidentally, more of which is deliberately started in an effort to re-stimulate growth. It is often possible to identify areas where former burning incidents occurred — here abrupt vegetation boundaries can be seen. To the undamaged side the heathers are tall and spreading, contrasting with the newly germinated, less woody plants growing where there has been a recent burn.

Bogbean

Menyanthes trifoliata

Bogbean is an important component in various types of shallow-water vegetation. It has spread into many parts of Ireland via the canal systems. Although many of these canals are now managed in a way that does not encourage the establishment and continuance of vegetation, there are still small colonies to be seen in some of the feeders. Bogbean has a huge, almost woody and very knobbly rooting system which forms a robust vegetative network in the mud on the edges of bogs and pools. This lattice provides support for other species whose natural habitat is in the transitional zone between open water and dry land. The large, three-lobed leaves stand clear of the water, to be followed by the flowers whose unusually fringed petals emerge from early summer on. The fruits are substantial structures, recognisable well into autumn, and seeds are produced in great numbers. The long-dead seeds, blackened and shining, are commonly preserved in layers within the bog peats, indicating the significant part played by Bogbean in the gradual infilling of the lakes thousands of years ago in the early stages of bog formation.

Bell Heather

Bogbean

Sea Holly

Eryngium maritimum

Sandhill systems have formed where there is an abundance of blown sand accumulating on the coast. For a large number of plants sandhills constitute their main habitat. Some of these species are confined to the coastal areas while others can find their way inland. Sea Holly is a large, glaucous-leaved, prickly plant, which forms dense colonies on undisturbed stretches of the sandy coast. The waxy finish on the leaves is a water-retention adaptation. When dry its twiggy stems snap easily and it is not able to cope with trampling by visitors or being driven over by cars. Many of the plants of the east coast are small, but on undamaged shores individual plants can be almost a metre wide and nearly as tall.

Pyramidal Orchid

Anacamptis pyramidalis

Lime-rich grasslands, when they are not mutilated beyond recognition, are rich in species, in colour and in associated insects. The most natural forms are those that have developed on the coast on sandhills and on exposures of glacial till. They have also formed where a thin covering of soil rests on the protruding limestone bedrock. Many of the esker grasslands of the midlands once also held large expanses of lime-rich grassland but these are severely threatened now by intensified agriculture, both pastoral and arable. Many of the species occur in each of these three major habitat types, signifying respectively their shared environmental requirements and characteristics. Pyramidal Orchid is a good bellwether species, often indicating the presence of a better type of limestone grassland with many typical associated plant species present in the colourful mix.

Marsh Woundwort

Stachys palustris

Marsh Woundwort is a widespread plant of wet, peaty ground, lake margins and drains. It can form extensive stands in low-grazing conditions with other tall species such as Common Valerian, *Valeriana officinalis*, Great Willowherb, *Epilobium hirsutum*, Meadowsweet, *Filipendula ulmaria*, and some of the larger grasses that can tolerate flooding. Indeed the occurrence of this species often indicates the former presence of much wetter conditions. In common with other emergent species, it has a substantial rooting system that can travel downwards in the soil profile as the water table falls. This disguises the fact that many smaller species that would have formerly grown with these species are completely unable to cope with this dense vegetation, where they are pressured for space and light as well as being unable to produce roots long enough to reach the falling water levels.

Autumn

Each autumn much of the biomass contained in the tree canopy transfers to ground level. Even in so-called evergreen forestry there is a steady fall of leaves, accelerating towards the end of the year. Twigs, cones, bark and leaves fall to the ground, to decay gradually. Decay in conifer systems is slow. Where sufficient light reaches the ground a limited shade-tolerant ground flora, usually of mosses, fungi and a few ferns, may gain a hold.

Fallow Deer

Dama dama
Fia buí

There can hardly be a more beautiful sight that that of Fallow Deer in their summer coat at the beginning of autumn. This is Ireland's most widespread deer because formerly it was held in up to 60 enclosed deer parks all over the country, from which it inevitably escaped or in some cases was released. It had been originally introduced to Ireland by the Normans and was traditionally maintained and managed in enclosures. For this reason the coat colour of Fallow Deer is much more variable than that of other species that had no such phase of prolonged, controlled breeding in their ancestry. Fallow Deer are the second largest of our deer and the males have characteristically broad palmate antlers.

Like all deer they are relatively shy creatures but in deer parks or protected areas where there is substantial human activity they become habituated to humans and may appear relatively tame. They are found in deciduous and mixed woodland particularly if they are in a mosaic with open grassland. They are highly social animals and may often congregate in large herds, although males and female live apart for most of the year and usually only come together during September, October and November. The rut takes place mainly in October. At this time males are extremely vocal and aggressive. They emit loud, staccato, cough-like belches and the sound of clashing antlers reverberates through the trees. Bucks fight by locking antlers, wrestling and pushing. Their antlers had begun growth the previous April when they shed their old pair. Throughout the summer the new antlers grew beneath a covering of furry skin and the bucks put on weight. By the end of August their antlers were fully grown, the overlying skin had died and was frayed off, they were close to their maximum weight and ready for battle. While the bucks were taking life easy, the does had given birth to their fawns in June and had spent the intervening period producing milk to fuel their rapid growth. They have to combine lactation with choosing a mate during the rut before returning to fawn-rearing. Thus in late autumn and early winter, while the bucks are again recovering from the exertions of the rut, the females are attempting to wean their fawns so that they can concentrate on providing nourishment for the fetus that is now growing within them.

Hart's-tongue Fern

Asplenium scolopendrium

In autumn the undersides of the fronds of Hart's-tongue Fern are covered with rusty-brown strips of sori. Each sorus contains spores which will eventually produce the next generation of plants. Hart's-tongue Fern grows typically on earthen banks in the core of hedgerows and on woodland margins on sloping banks. It can also grow on shaded rocks, especially on protruding limestone boulders, and has made its way into cities, often living with other ferns on old shaded walls, especially near leaking drainpipes. In its natural habitats it is an elegant plant, unfurling its fronds as spring advances in the way that many larger ferns do. These toughen up through the summer and by autumn are mature. The individuals growing on old walls in cities are seldom so graceful.

Great Skua

Stercorarius skua
Meirleach mór

Each autumn sees the migration of skuas from breeding grounds in northern Europe to their wintering areas off Africa. Their migration routes take them out into the north Atlantic and south past Ireland. Depending on weather conditions, they can be seen in large numbers off our coastline. The commonest and largest of these gull-like species is the Great Skua (or Bonxie as they are often called). This species breeds in Scotland and Iceland but has also bred on remote islands off the west coast of Ireland. Skuas are best described as being avian pirates. Instead of searching for their own food, they will chase, terrorise and rob other seabirds of their food. They specialise in relentlessly chasing other birds to such an extent that the pursued often regurgitate their last meal in an attempt to terminate the chase. This Great Skua, photographed off Kerry, has just started to chase the Lesser Black-backed Gull. The terrified look in the gull speaks for itself, and moments later the skua was rewarded for its efforts with a regurgitated meal!

Sabine's Gull

Xemas sabini
Sléibhín Sabine

This beautifully marked, small gull is a bird of the high Arctic regions of Canada, Greenland and Spitzbergen. Each autumn birds migrate south to wintering quarters in the southern hemisphere where they spend the season far out at sea. Sabine's Gulls are seen off Ireland following strong Atlantic storms and gale force winds that blow the birds across to the western seaboard of Europe. Birds will also follow trawlers at sea in search of offal and this may bring them closer inshore. In late autumn many of the Sabine's Gulls encountered are browner, immature birds, but in early autumn it is possible to encounter some adults in full summer plumage. This adult was photographed at sea 10km west of the Blasket Islands, Kerry. It was one of five adult Sabine's Gulls that stayed with our boat for over two hours.

Snowberry

Symphoricarpos albus

Snowberry was introduced to Ireland as a garden plant because of its bright white berries which add a touch of colour in autumn. Its natural home is in North America. It produces small, inconspicuous, pink flowers earlier in the year. It has become naturalised in many parts of Ireland and was one of the first of a large number of invasive species to exert a negative influence on our natural habitats. It has spread by suckering from old gardens and can even form dense thickets in ornamental woodland. At some sites it has persisted in hedges long after the original homestead gardens in which it was planted have disappeared.

Fly Agaric

Amanita muscaria

Fungi can grow spectacularly fast and many species grow particularly well in conifer woodlands. Fly Agaric is the typical fairyland fungus. Despite its attractive appearance it is poisonous and has disturbing psychoactive properties.

Wood Mouse

Apodemus sylvaticus
Luch (luchóg) fhéir

The Wood Mouse is one of Ireland's most numerous and widespread mammals and is found in woodland, hedgerows, arable fields, boglands, heather, sand-dunes and gardens. It breeds mostly between April and October. As a result, in early spring, populations of Wood Mice are at their lowest. This is of concern to more than Wood Mice. Ireland has relatively few species of small rodents or indeed of small terrestrial mammals in general and so a great burden falls upon the Wood Mouse. It is a major component of the diet of Long-eared Owls, Barn Owls, Kestrels, foxes, stoats, Pine Martens, Badgers and Feral and Domestic Cats. Thus this engaging little animal is under almost continuous assault from the air and the ground. It is a tribute to its hardiness and resilience that it can sustain such an important ecological role. Although it is a gnawer, it is quite opportunistic and will eat mainly seeds but also nuts, fruit, seedlings, buds, fungi, snails, insects, even earthworms. In times of plenty it often creates food stores in secluded spots within its home range.

The Wood Mouse has a more appealing demeanour than the House Mouse that seems somewhat furtive by comparison. The Wood Mouse is an inquisitive little rodent with large eyes and ears and a longish tail. It has the habit of suddenly leaping into the air when startled. The coat is dark brown on the back, yellowish-brown on the flanks and off-white underneath. It is not often seen because it is mostly nocturnal but is often active for a few hours after dawn and before dusk.

Ireland's Wood Mice have a cosmopolitan ancestry. Although they are not as intimately associated with humans as the House Mouse, they were among the earliest mammals to hitch-hike into Ireland with the first human colonists. They have since been joined by others who came with the Vikings and later invaders.

In late autumn a clear view of what is intended by mixed woodland emerges. Some broadleaved species are still green. Others have already lost all their leaves, despite the shelter provided by the taller species. The occasional conifer stands above the canopy of deciduous trees and other broad-leaved evergreen species retain their leaves. Depending on the species mix and age structure of the woods, the leaf-litter mix will vary as will the amount of light reaching the floor.

Black-tailed Godwit

Limosa limosa
Guilbneach earrdhubh

A common wader of estuaries and mudflats, Black-tailed Godwits are a very rare breeding bird in Ireland. The majority of the birds seen in Ireland arrive from their breeding grounds in Iceland by early autumn. Like many waders, godwits use their long bills to probe into the soft mud in search of worms, molluscs and larvae. Their bills have highly sensitive tips and the birds feel for their food instead of finding it by sight. Black-tailed Godwits show a rich chestnut plumage in summer, ideal for camouflage when nesting on the ground. In winter they turn grey and white which is a plumage ideally suited for remaining inconspicuous on the grey mudflats. This young bird was feeding on exposed tidal mudflats at Swords, Dublin.

Dunlin

Calidris alpina
Breacóg

Ireland has a small breeding population of Dunlin based in western and north-western regions, but in the early weeks of autumn we see a marked increase in the population as birds arrive from breeding grounds in Iceland and Europe. Found in large numbers on coastal estuaries, mudflats and lakes, Dunlin flocks often host passage migrant birds such as Curlew Sandpipers and Little Stints as well as rare North American species. By autumn adults show very worn plumage and begin to moult into their winter grey-and-white plumage. This adult, photographed at Tacumshin Lake, Wexford, is showing extreme wear to its plumage.

Leisler's Bat

Nyctalus leisleri
Ialtóg Leisler

This is Ireland's largest breeding bat and it is found throughout most of the country. It is probably our third most common bat and Ireland has more of them that any other European country. It appears more shaggy than Ireland's other bats because of the longer fur around its shoulders and back.

In Ireland Leisler's Bats may be seen on the wing between March and October. They hibernate probably in hollow trees or niches and cavities in buildings. During the active season, Leisler's Bats emerge from their summer roosts relatively early in the evening just before or round about sunset. If the light is particularly strong such as on a cloudless night with a full moon they tend to emerge later. Nevertheless sometimes early hunting Leisler's Bats and late hunting Swallows and Swifts may all be on the wing at the same time. It has long, narrow, relatively pointed wings, typical of a fast flier. Its flight path tends to be faster, higher and straighter than the remainder of our bats. It can often be seen flying swiftly at the level of treetops, over scrub and sometimes in the open, making smooth swoops or turns. It often forages around street lamps and sometimes over water. It does not appear to be particularly manoeuvrable and cannot easily pick prey directly off vegetation.

Leisler's Bats are prepared to travel up to 10km from their home roost to a feeding area. They locate prey by emitting high frequency sounds (mostly inaudible to humans) and listen for the echo if they bounce off an insect in the vicinity. The frequencies they use are best for detecting medium-sized insects such as moths, caddis flies, crane flies and beetles but they will also feed on smaller insects if they are swarming at densities high enough to be detected. Analysis of their droppings can reveal what type of prey they have been taking. This shows that most of their diet consists of beetles and dung flies, with variable amounts of midges.

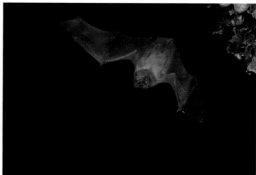

Curlew Sandpiper

Calidris ferruginea
Gobadán crotaigh

Arriving with flocks of Dunlin, Curlew Sandpipers are autumn passage migrants. Breeding in Siberia, many young birds migrate along the western fringes of Europe, stopping off to feed on the way. They are found along most coastal counties in early autumn but, unlike the Dunlin which winter here, Curlew Sandpipers continue south to spend the winter in Southern Africa. By late October most have departed, but on occasions some do over-winter here. This young bird was with a small flock of Dunlin at Gormanstown, Meath. It had just finished preening and is clearly showing the white rump, one of the features that distinguish them from Dunlin.

Ruff

Philomachus pugnax
Rufachán

An uncommon but regular autumn migrant from Europe, Ruffs are found along the muddy verges of coastal, freshwater and brackish pools and mudflats. The species derives its name from the large ruff of neck feathers that adult males show during the breeding season when they gather in communal leks to display to females. These adornments are lost after the breeding season. Males are considerably larger than females which are called Reeves. In autumn most birds seen are young birds passing through Ireland on their way to wintering grounds farther south. Some birds occasionally over-winter. Young birds show a striking pattern of feathering on their upperparts and buff-coloured underparts. This young male was feeding on the mudflats at Swords, Dublin.

Common Sandpiper

Actitis hypoleucos
Gobadán

Common Sandpiper is unusual among our wader species in that it is a summer visitor to Ireland where most others are either resident breeding birds, passage migrants or winter visitors. They are a common and widespread breeding species found along rocky streams, rivers and lakeshores. By late summer and early autumn, adults and young birds move from the breeding grounds and are found along coastal wetlands. They are joined by birds migrating from Britain and northern Europe. By late autumn they depart to spend the winter in Africa. This young bird was feeding on the mudflats of the Broadmeadows Estuary, Swords, Dublin.

Bracken

Pteridium aquilinum

Bracken is a large species of fern, usually most obvious on higher ground where rough pasture has become neglected or abandoned. In these circumstances it forms dense, aggregated colonies covering large tracts of land where it acts as a form of woodland substitute, its dense shading fronds emulating a low-level forest canopy. It can also grow in older, leached sand-dunes, drying-out bog margins and in birch and oak woodland. Indeed many woodland-margin species such as Bluebell, Primrose and Ground Ivy can thrive under Bracken but not in adjoining pastures, not only because of reduced grazing pressures but also because of the shelter provided by the Bracken. The term 'Bracken' has become a generalised landscape descriptor to mean rough upland ground. Bracken has recently been portrayed as an invasive species but in many cases it would more accurately be seen as a species that is reclaiming its natural territory, spreading back from hedges and field boundaries onto land that was cleared and maintained by earlier generations of farmers.

Buff-breasted Sandpiper

Tryngites subruficollis
Gobadán broinn-donnbhuí

Pectoral Sandpiper
Calidris melanotos
Gobadán uchtach

Buff-breasted Sandpipers and Pectoral Sandpipers are breeding species from the High Arctic regions of North America. Each autumn these birds, migrating at high altitudes along the eastern seaboard of North America en-route to their wintering grounds in South America, get swept across the Atlantic and make landfall in Europe. Being on the western fringes of Europe, Ireland is ideally located to attract them and both species are regular autumn visitors. It is interesting to note that in the majority of cases the birds seen in Europe are young birds undertaking their first migrations. Being High Arctic species, they will rarely have encountered humans and, as a result, are known for their tameness. In some years small flocks of ten or more Buff-breasted Sandpipers can be found at one location. These are birds that are more at home on dry, short-grass areas while Pectoral Sandpipers prefer the muddy edges of reed-fringed pools and wetlands. Both images were captured at Tacumshin Lake, Wexford.

Rivers in spate are severe environments for broad-leaved plants. The shearing effect of water, reinforced by the constant abrasion of mobile sand and gravel, rips many plants to shreds once the rivers begin to fill again in autumn. Most plants that survive here must do so in the sheltering lee of larger boulders. However, a large number of moss and liverwort species are adapted for life here, putting on some growth and spore-producing capsules when water levels are lower. Many of these riverine species can cope with extended periods of inundation and for several mosses and liverworts this is their preferred home. There are even some truly aquatic mosses. Some of the mosses that live here develop extraordinarily strong, almost wiry stems that can cope with the harsh environment but most do best hidden from the torrent on the sheltered side of the larger rocks.

Red Deer

Cervus elaphus
Fia rua

There can be no sound more redolent of the turning of the year than the deep rumbling roar of the Red Deer stag as it enters the rut. Throughout the long summer days, while the hinds have been rearing their calves, the stags have been accumulating muscle, storing fat and growing a new set of antlers to replace the set shed last March. In September they leave the bachelor groups in which they spent the summer, and move onto the areas where the females have spent the summer. By now their antlers are fully grown, the nourishing skin which enveloped them has died and been frayed and they are now ready for battle. Most have waited for six years for this opportunity and for many it may be their last.

Each rutting stag attempts to gather a harem of hinds, usually a group of related females of several generations, that share the same area. He is a jealous and attentive consort and attempts to keep the harem together and defend it against all comers. Fighting is extremely dangerous for stags and they have evolved a ritual for settling disputes. They roar to issue or to answer a challenge and higher status stags roar louder, longer and more often. If this does not settle matters then they escalate to a closer approach in which they walk close together in parallel in a display of size. If the matter is still unresolved antlers are engaged, often with a loud clash, and a pushing and wrestling contest begins. Conflict is at its height in early October. Hinds are somewhat choosy in respect of a stag with whom they will mate, but in general, successful control of a harem usually guarantees reproduction for a small fraction of the males. By the middle of November most of the fertile hinds will have conceived and the stags, who have scarcely eaten for over a month, will have lost up to 20 per cent of their body weight. The sexes now tend to go their separate ways, the females to gestate their growing calf and the male to recover from the rigours of the rut.

As river and lake levels rise after the summer, various taller species that have gained a roothold earlier continue to grow, keeping pace with the rising waters and usually exceeding it. In time these colonies of emergent vegetation will consolidate to form dense, impenetrable beds of reeds and sometime later, willow scrub. Sand, gravel and vegetable debris will gradually accumulate, causing local infilling of the water and a new, muddy soil to form. Later, other emergent species will become established in these more stable conditions, all able to withstand the exigencies of fluctuating water levels, and to flower and set fruit when levels are lower. True aquatics, their leaves submerged or floating, can rise and fall as the levels change and can produce flowers and fruit both above and below the water. Many of the larger sedge species are able to form substantial tussocks that stand above the water, even in winter floods.

Oystercatcher

Haematopus ostralegus
Roilleach

A common, resident breeding species found in all coastal areas, Oystercatchers are best recognised by their striking black-and-white plumage and long orange bill. In autumn our population increases with the arrival of birds from Europe. With so many birds beginning to flock together, it seems that many pairs, still in breeding mode, can remain quite territorial and will defend their boundaries against these new arrivals. Such territorial displays involve synchronised marches along the border of the territory, giving loud, trilling, piping calls. In this image, the channel obviously marks the territorial boundary and the pair is engaging the bird at the top in such a territorial display. The image was taken at Gormanstown Beach, Meath.

Chiffchaff

Phylloscopus collybita
Tiuf-teaf

One of our commonest breeding warblers, Chiffchaffs derive their name from their repeated *chiff-chaff* song. Arriving in Ireland in early spring, they are among the first migrants to reach our shores each year. Chiffchaffs breed in a wide variety of habitats, from hedgerows and scrub to mature woodland. They build nests in deep cover just above ground level. By autumn our breeding birds are on the move south to the wintering grounds in north Africa and can be found on coastal islands and headlands. Numbers increase as the autumn season progresses, with birds moving through Ireland from more northern breeding areas in Europe. By late October most Chiffchaffs have departed but a very small number can over-winter in Ireland. This bird was photographed on Inishbofin, Galway.

Grey Seal

Haliochoerus gryphus
Rón mór

Most Grey Seal cows in Ireland give birth in October, normally on exposed rocky shores or on sand bars near deep water. They usually have traditional breeding grounds where they may assemble in large numbers. Twins are extremely rare and the single pup is quite large, about 14kg at birth. Not only are pups large at birth but they also grow rapidly and put on up to 2kg per day. This growth is fuelled by milk which may consist of up to 40 per cent fat (about eight to ten times richer than that of dairy cows) and which they receive about every six hours. Nevertheless, life for a seal pup is quite precarious. Some are lost by being washed out to sea during storms and other are accidentally killed if the colony is particularly crowded. When pups are weaned after about three to four weeks they weigh over 40kg, of which up to 16kg may be fat. This is crucial for two reasons. Firstly, a layer of fat under the skin insulates the pup which, like all small mammals, is particularly prone to heat loss because of the large area of skin relative to its weight. Secondly, although pups can and may swim within two weeks of birth it takes about three weeks before they are sufficiently skilful to be able to catch their own food. The fat they have stored while being suckled tides them over this lean spell.

The tremendous effort at milk production also takes its toll on the females and they may lose a quarter of their body weight before the pup is weaned. There is little rest, however, when maternal duties are over, because the females come into breeding condition as soon as the pups are weaned. While the females have been busy giving birth and lactating, the males have also been busy staking claim to areas of beach that already contain females or that are close by. Fighting by males may be frequent and severe because, although the risks are high, the rewards are great. A few males will father most of next year's pups and many males fail to breed throughout their life. Some pups are accidentally killed by enraged bulls during the chaos that occasionally ensues during the breeding season. So preoccupied are the bulls with mating that they may not feed for up to eight weeks. When the cows mate they leave the colony soon after. Although they carry a fertilised egg, little happens for several months (14–18 weeks). The fertilised egg undergoes a few cycles of cell division until it becomes a ball of about 32 or 64 cells. At this point development is arrested until the spring, when the ball of cells implants in the wall of the uterus and the fetus begins to develop. This delay of implantation adjusts when gestation really begins and allows the pup to be ready for birth about 31–34 weeks later, next October.

Starling

Sturnus vulgaris
Druid

A common, widespread and very familiar bird in Ireland, Starlings are found in a wide range of habitats, from towns and cities to farmland, woodland and shorelines. In autumn the population increases with the arrival of birds from northern and central Europe. By late autumn and early winter, birds can form enormous roosting flocks using reedbeds and woodlands to roost communally. In summer Starlings appear quite black and glossy, have little or no spotting, and show yellow bills. However, following their post-breeding moult, they acquire their striking winter plumage of dazzling white spots. When seen in good sunlight, this plumage is further enhanced by the wonderful iridescence of purples, blues and greens of the birds' feathers. This Starling was photographed in evening sunlight, on Mizen Head, Cork.

Arctic Warbler

Phylloscopus borealis
Ceolaire Artach

Besides the migration of common summer visitors, Ireland can also play host to birds that stray off course on their autumn migrations. Many of these birds can be blown in the wrong direction as they migrate south out of Europe. Others, especially young birds, may simply fly in the wrong direction. This Arctic Warbler, for example, is a northern Scandinavian breeding species and winters in south-east Asia. It was present on Cape Clear Island, Cork, for almost two weeks. When it arrived it was thin and weak, and spent much of its time feeding actively, attempting to restore its fat reserves to enable it to continue migrating. How such birds reach Ireland is the subject of much debate. One theory suggests that they reverse migrate. This implies that the birds head north-west instead of south-east in autumn; migrating in the reverse direction. Such a theory may explain how this bird, which should have been in the warm climate of south-east Asia, was feeding in a garden in south-west Ireland.

Wheatear

Oenanthe oenanthe
Clochrán

A common summer visitor, Wheatears are found on open ground in habitats ranging from mountains and farmland to coastal pastures and islands. In spring Wheatears are often the first migrant to arrive into Ireland from wintering grounds in Africa. Dispersing from the coast, they move to their breeding territories. Nesting in holes in walls, among rocks and even in rabbit burrows, a pair can raise two families in a season. By early autumn the first birds return to the coast in preparation for their southward migration. Birds that breed in Greenland and Canada also winter in Africa and are renowned for being among the world's greatest migrants, undertaking a non-stop flight of over 2,400km across the Atlantic Ocean in less than 30 hours. This young Wheatear was photographed at Carnsore Point, Wexford.

Birch thrives on damp, ungrazed, slightly acid land. It is a fast-growing species and can invade abandoned land rapidly and form small copses. It has recently colonised many cut-away bog margins and a number of ferns and coarse grasses can grow beneath its canopy. Unfortunately birch can also invade sites of high conservation value, converting species-rich wetlands into woodlands where most of the distinctive and rarer species are eventually crowded or shaded out.

Bank Vole

Myodes glareolus
Luch rua/Vól bruaigh

The Bank Vole is an attractive little rodent with chestnut-brown fur. At present it is unlikely that one will encounter a Bank Vole north of a line approximately from Mayo to Kildare, but it will not long be so. This little rodent, Ireland's only vole, appeared in the country sometime in the second quarter of the 20th century, on the southern side of the Shannon estuary, and it was first recognised here in the 1960s. It has been spreading steadily since its arrival and will have colonised the whole island within about 15 years or so.

The Bank Vole is more compact than the Field Mouse and has a noticeably shorter tail and smaller ears and eyes. Unlike mice they tend to be active by day and night and are more placid and rather less excitable that Wood Mice. They prefer to live in dense undergrowth, in woods, in hedgerows, scrub or rank grasslands. They breed between April and October and population densities are highest in autumn when there may be more than 30 per hectare.

Bank Voles are largely vegetarian and feed mainly on berries, roots, bulbs, seeds, fruit and fungi, as well as on leaves and grasses. The also eat snails, earthworms and insect larvae. In winter, if food is particularly scarce, they may strip the bark from young trees and saplings to get at the soft tissue underneath. This brings them into conflict with foresters, but the damage is usually short-lived and localised.

Ireland has rather few native small rodents and not surprisingly Bank Voles soon came to the attention of a variety of predators. In the south of the country they are preyed on by foxes, Kestrels and Barn Owls.

Swallow

Hirundo rustica
Fáinleog

Probably one of Ireland's best-known migrants, the sight of the first Swallow each spring is often considered as the harbinger of summer. Wintering in South Africa, the birds migrate over the Sahara Desert and reach Ireland by early spring. Studies have shown that birds return to the exact same barn, shed or outhouse that they were born in the previous year and can return to breed at the same location for several years. Building strong nests of mud pellets and grass, the birds often just need to repair and line their nests upon their return. Here a pair can raise as many as three broods in a single season. Young birds leave the nest when they are just three weeks old and are fed by their parents for a further two weeks. At five weeks old, they are fully independent birds and disperse away from the breeding grounds. By early autumn large numbers of Swallows can gather along southern coastal headlands and wetlands, awaiting favourable migration weather. By late October Swallows have left the country and many will already have reached their wintering grounds 10,000km to the south. These young Swallows were in Cleggan, Galway, and were obviously part of a late brood. They were sitting patiently on a ship's rope in the harbour, waiting for their parents to return to feed them.

Spindle

Euonymus europaeus

Spindle is a very inconspicuous shrub or small tree through summer. It has small, greenish-white flowers and its leaves are much the same colour as most other hedgerow and woodland shrubs. However, as autumn approaches the leaves begin to turn reddish but remain on the trees in this condition for several months. Much more spectacularly, the fruits develop around this time — four distinct, non-fleshy, pinkish lobes surrounding a bright orange centre. Spindle is typical of dry, lime-rich ground and is therefore much more common in the Irish midlands, especially associated with roadside hedgerows in esker country.

Little Blue Heron

Egretta caerulea

Common Nighthawk

Chordeiles minor

In some autumns Ireland is graced by the presence of avian superstars and there are none greater than birds that somehow have managed to cross the Atlantic Ocean from North America. Encountering birds in Ireland that you know should be migrating to southern regions of the United States or Central and South America is a rare privilege. Unlike geese and some waders, these birds are not designed for such oceanic crossings but this can happen when the birds are migrating along the eastern seaboard of North America. If they are unfortunate, they can encounter strong Atlantic depressions that sweep them up and carry them towards Europe. As with the occurrence of waders from North America, Ireland's position on the western fringes of Europe makes it one of the first locations these weary travellers meet as they arrive in off the sea.

The Little Blue Heron was photographed at Letterfrack, Galway. It was the first time this species had occurred in Ireland and drew many visitors from all parts of Ireland and Britain. Young birds show this white, Little Egret-like plumage, but as they mature they show a blue-grey plumage.

The Common Nighthawk was seen near Caherciveen, Kerry. Related to Nightjars, this bird was found hawking insects around gardens following several days of severe Atlantic storms. That any of these birds survive such amazing journeys is a testimony to their endurance and survival instincts.

Dog Rose

Rosa canina

The destruction of most of the Irish woodlands was slightly compensated for by hedging the surviving pastoral and arable landscape. In many areas hedges were simply planted across existing open countryside — in other areas fragments of scrub woodland were incorporated into hedge systems or were used as sources of trees and bushes for planting into hedges. Certain species then spread by seed from existing natural sources into planted hedges. Most of the species that grow in hedges are woodland margin plants — in this case some of the many subspecies and forms of Dog Rose, *Rosa canina*. The hedgerow is an ideal habitat for woodland margin species — well lit and, in the case of the roadside verge hedges, ungrazed — at least on one side. As a result a distinct set of species has developed which are now more common in hedges than in the nearby woodlands — if any such features have survived at local level. Dog Roses were discovered during the Second World War to be a significant source of vitamin C and were subsequently utilised as a vital food supplement when it was impossible to provide Britain and Ireland with fresh oranges. Various commercially-produced elixirs such as Rose Hip syrup were purchasable in chemist shops. In recent years their dietary function has been supplanted by capsules and fizzy tablets.

As lake levels fall from the end of summer onwards a new habitat is revealed. Muds, submerged sands and pebbly shores are exposed. Various short-lived plants, usually fast-growing annuals, spring into life, germinating from seeds that have lain dormant from the previous year. These will grow, flower and set new seed in the few months of opportunity before water levels rise again. This muddy zone, both transitory and transitional, between dry ground and open water is also occupied by a number of ephemeral mosses and liverworts geared to flourish in this area. Furthermore, many insects, especially small ground beetles, sometimes in their thousands, hunt among the gravels for even smaller insects of the waterline.

Muntjac

Muntiacus reevesi
Muntiac

The Muntjac is one of the latest mammals to arrive in Ireland. It has been reliably reported from Wicklow and Wexford but little is known of its distribution. It is also unclear whether the reports relate to animals deliberately imported and released, or to animals that escaped from private collections. It seems likely that more than one release, deliberate or otherwise, is involved. In fact it is not clear which species of Muntjac is involved but it is almost certainly the Chinese Muntjac which has become well-established in southern England. We can expect it to spread and become established in Ireland also.

The Muntjac is a small, generally solitary deer with a rather hunched appearance that skulks in dense undergrowth, thickets and scrub. It is about as large as an Irish setter dog. It preferentially feeds on leaves, fruit and nuts of trees and shrubs for most of the year and on grasses in late spring and summer. Probably as a result of its sub-tropical origin, the Muntjac does not have a breeding season and its young may be born at any time of the year. It can sometimes breed twice within a 13-month period and produces one fawn per gestation.

Fungi

Fungi of various sorts comprise an amazing variety of shapes and colours. They develop rapidly from a system of mycelium which grows underground, through leaf-litter or within decaying wood. What we see are their fruiting bodies — structures that erupt, grow rapidly and decay almost as fast. Fungi are vital in the process of breaking down and recycling natural products, especially in woodlands, but many species can be encountered in sand-dunes, especially in winter, in lawns, not only as the mushrooms but as the familiar fairy rings, in houses as mould on bread, cheese and dry rot.

Magpie

Pica pica
Snag breac

One of Ireland's commonest and most familiar species, Magpies are a highly adaptable and successful species. Found throughout the whole country in a wide variety of habitats, they have gained a bad reputation for taking eggs and young nestlings of many species of birds. They are of course opportunistic and will feed on any food available, from discarded rubbish to insects, carrion and seeds. However, the Magpie captured in this image which was taken on Inishbofin, Galway, had developed a whole new concept in takeaway food. It spent up to ten minutes on the back and around the head of the white sheep and was removing ticks from the animal. The sheep was totally unconcerned and eventually sat down and seemed to be enjoying the experience. A black sheep, feeding nearby, noticed this activity. It walked up and stood close by, observing the proceedings. When the Magpie had finished removing ticks from the white sheep, it then moved onto the black sheep and performed its grooming service for it. It spent another ten minutes feeding off that sheep before flying off.

Sea Aster

In autumn when tides are at their lowest, a new coastal habitat becomes visible. On the area between the lowest salt marsh vegetation and the permanently wet open sea a fringe of salt-tolerant species occurs that are able to tolerate extended periods of inundation. These are the Saltworts, *Salicornia* species, plants that are equipped with thick, fleshy stems and branches where water is stored. They have minute flowers, little more than clusters of tiny stamens pressed against the stems and branches of the plant. Different species of Saltwort inhabit different sections of the shore. Dense, almost finger-like, branched plants are typical of the lowest stretches of the shore while taller, more freely branched species should be searched for at higher levels.

Higher up on the salt marsh different species dominate. The most conspicuous of the taller plants is Sea Aster, *Aster tripolium*, a plant that can be often almost 80cm tall, surmounted by dense clusters of daisy-like flowers but blue and individually larger. In this zone it grows with Thrift and Scurvy-grass, but these have usually gone into seed by the time the flowers of Sea Aster begin to open. This is a common coastal plant especially along the estuarine salt marshes and can spread along rivers far from the open sea, its presence indicating the upper limits of tidal influence. It is also a feature of shaded sea cliffs and rocky shores. It is the only native Irish Aster, but there are many other species that have been expelled from gardens and are now becoming established not only on waste ground, but also in the wild, especially on river banks.

Holly

Ilex aquifolium

As winter approaches the berries of Holly begin to redden. The flowers — small, greenish-white, four-petalled constructions — are often overlooked and should be looked for from June on. Though usually encountered as a shrub, it can form a tall tree, and some of our older hedge boundaries, especially those on townland boundaries, often have large examples. Some of these hedges, especially in the lowlands, may even be remnants of more ancient woodland long since eliminated from the landscape. On higher ground Holly is more common, often forming scrub or even standing alone on windswept hillsides where few other shrubs can survive. Many cultivars of holly have been developed by horticulturists.

Winter

Red-throated Diver

Gavia stellata
Lóma rua

Though a rare breeding species, Red-throated Divers are a common winter visitor from Iceland and northern Europe. In summer they are found nesting on small, remote islets on loughs and lakes in northern regions. However, in winter they are found on open coastal water, bays and harbours. As their name suggests, they dive for fish but only show their red throats in summer plumage. In winter they are dark above and white below. This winter-plumaged bird, photographed inside Dún Laoghaire harbour, Dublin, is just starting to moult and is showing the first signs of the red throat of summer plumage.

Brent Goose

Branta bernicla
Cadhan

A common winter visitor from breeding grounds in Arctic Canada and Greenland, Brent Geese are found in large flocks in many coastal areas. Feeding on marine vegetation, the birds will also feed on grass and are now a regular visitor to suburban football pitches. Arriving into Ireland during early autumn, the birds can remain until late April or early May. Our birds are of the pale-bellied race which differ from birds that visit other parts of Europe. Those birds, breeding in Siberia, are known as Dark-bellied Brent and show, as their name suggests, a darker lower breast and belly. Breeding success is easily monitored each season when the birds return to Ireland as young birds show clear, pale edges to the upperpart feathers. Arriving to the wintering grounds with their parents, the young birds stay with the adults until spring, by which time they will have learned where the best winter feeding locations are. This young bird was photographed on the North Bull Island, Dublin.

Sika Deer

Cervus nippon
Fia Seapánach

Winter and early spring are difficult times for deer. The stags have used up almost all their reserves during the rut in the autumn and must face a time of food shortage with little margin for error. They still retain their magnificent antlers grown during the time of plenty the previous summer, but their bodies have lost their bulk and the neck muscles, swollen and enlarged the previous autumn, have now shrunk and the animals recycle the protein to cope with food shortage. Soon even the antlers, that cost so much to grow, will be shed and the stags will look a sorry sight until they begin to replenish their reserves and put on condition. As part of the annual renewal the process of growing a new set will begin again and will not be complete until late August.

The hinds too are showing the strain. They may still be attempting to wean their calf, born the previous May or June, and already a new fetus is growing within their body. Gone are the sleek, rounded curves of the summer and they are more gaunt and angular. By now quite a few who were unable to meet the demands of a hungry calf will have lost it to the cold and wet weather. Soon both stags and hinds will shed their greyish winter coat, which gives them a somewhat bedraggled appearance. The summer coat of the Sika Deer is much lighter and ranges from chestnut reddish brown to dark brown, and rows of white spots scarcely distinguishable in the winter coat are revealed in all their glory. Their white tail and rump appears even more striking in summer.

Nevertheless Sika Deer cope well with Irish conditions. They evolved on the Japanese islands and were introduced to Europe in 1860 when Lord Powerscourt imported four individuals to his deer park at Powerscourt. From there they were donated to other estates from which they accidentally or deliberately were released. So well have they prospered that they may be, although not our most widespread, probably our most abundant deer. Quite apart from the effect of their browsing on forests, Sika Deer represent an unforeseen threat to Ireland's Red Deer. Although biologists were convinced that Sika and Red are different species, they never developed barriers to inbreeding. As a result, they can and did cross-breed in Powerscourt and most of the Sika Deer in Wicklow, who are descended from escapees, have some genes derived from Red Deer. This has so far not occurred elsewhere in Ireland as far as we know.

Gadwall

Anas strepera
Gadual

A scarce breeding species and uncommon winter visitor from Iceland and Europe, Gadwall are found on freshwater lakes and wetlands. They feed by grazing on aquatic vegetation and seeds. Because of this, they are known as dabbling ducks and often upend, putting their tails in the air as they reach under the water to feed on the vegetation below. Drakes appear plain grey at the distance but, when seen well, they reveal a complex pattern of dark crescent shapes and lines on the body called vermiculations. Many species of ducks show these vermiculations. In flight Gadwalls show a striking, white patch on the wing called a speculum; most dabbling ducks show a speculum, with each species having a unique colour combination. This drake was photographed in Strangford Lough, Down.

Wigeon

Anas penelope
Rualacha

A common winter visitor from Iceland, Scandinavia and Siberia, Wigeon are found on coastal estuaries, lakes, marshes and wetlands throughout Ireland. Besides their striking plumage males also give a very loud, plaintive, whistling call. Another of our dabbling ducks, Wigeon eat a variety of aquatic vegetation and seeds as well as grass near coastal locations. Wigeon arrive into Ireland by late autumn and can form large flocks in winter. They depart by early spring but have bred here on a few occasions. This drake was photographed on Strangford Lough, Down.

Red-breasted Merganser

Mergus serrator
Síolta rua

Red-breasted Mergansers are a common, resident species, breeding on inland lakes and large river systems. In winter they are also found along coastal areas and can be seen inside harbours, in estuaries and on the open sea. A diving duck, Red-breasted Mergansers feed on a variety of small fish and invertebrates. Their long, narrow bill has small serrations along the cutting edge and, for this reason, they belong to a family of ducks collectively known as sawbills. Both males and females show the long, wispy head crests. In late winter males perform courtship dances to attract the females. This drake was photographed at Malahide, Dublin.

After the winter storms many branches, twigs and small trees will have fallen to the ground. In time these parts, as well as the leaves of autumn, will be recycled, being broken down by bacteria, fungi and invertebrate action. In more natural woodlands, on sloping soils, leaf litter gathers behind boulders and logs, in depressions and at the damper base of lower slopes. It is this structural complexity that makes for the expression of true natural diversity, where different species occupy the niches that are most appropriate for their individual life forms and styles.

Redshank

Tringa totanus
Cosdeargán

Greenshank

Tringa nebularia
Laidhrín glas

Redshanks are a common, resident species, breeding in small numbers in some midland and northern regions of Ireland. In winter our population increases with the arrival of birds from Iceland and Europe and the species is found in all coastal and some midland areas of the country. As the name suggests, they are best recognised by their bright, orange-red legs. Greenshanks are a very rare breeding species and are usually seen from late autumn as birds migrate from Europe to spend the winter in Ireland. Larger and less numerous than Redshanks, they derive their names from their greenish-coloured legs which can be seen as this bird wades through deep but calm water. Like most waders, the long bills allow the birds to probe into the soft ground in search of larvae and worms. Both images were captured in Dublin — the Redshank on the North Bull Island and the Greenshank at the Swords Estuary.

Curlew

Numenius arquata
Crotach

Our largest wader, Curlews are perhaps best known for their plaintive, rolling, *cur-lee* calls which can be heard both in summer and in winter. A scarce breeding species found on remote upland bogs, wet meadows and farmlands, habitat loss and drainage has resulted in a serious decline in the Irish breeding population in recent years. In winter, numbers increase with the arrival of birds from Britain and northern Europe and they are found in all regions. The long bill is ideal for probing deep into soft grasslands or the mud of our coastal estuaries in search of worms. Despite their size, they can be very inconspicuous, their plumage providing ideal camouflage. This bird was photographed on the North Bull Island, Dublin.

Turnstone

Arenaria interpres
Piardálai trá

A very common winter visitor from Greenland, Iceland and northern Europe, Turnstones are found along rocky shorelines and seaweed-strewn beaches as well as around piers and harbours. As their name suggests, the birds flick over stones, rocks and seaweed in search of larvae, insects and small crustaceans. In summer the birds show rich, chestnut-coloured upperparts which gives them their alternative name of Ruddy Turnstone. In winter the plumage is duller, allowing the birds to remain well camouflaged. This bird was photographed at Annagassan, Louth. It was searching for insects under large shells on the beach.

Iceland Gull

Larus glaucoides
Faoileán Íoslannach

Iceland Gulls are an uncommon winter visitor to Irish fishing ports and harbours. Despite their name, they actually breed in Greenland. In some winters they and other northern breeding gulls move south into the Atlantic and feed on waste from trawlers they encounter far out at sea. The gulls will frequently follow the fishing fleet to shore, and in some years large numbers of 'northern gulls' can be found around busy fishing ports such as Killybegs in Donegal. Like many large gulls, the birds take up to four years to mature, changing from the pale coffee-coloured plumage of young birds to the grey-backed, white-winged plumage of adults. By late spring most will move north again to their breeding grounds. This young Iceland Gull was photographed in Baltimore Harbour, Cork.

Short-eared Owl

Asio flammeus
Ulchabhán réisc

A scarce winter visitor from Iceland and northern Europe, Short-eared Owls differ from most owl species by being a diurnal hunter. Rarely perching in trees, they prefer to sit on the ground or on low perches and hunt by silently quartering over rough pastures, moorlands and stubble fields as well as coastal sand-dunes and marshes in search of rats and mice. Where available, the birds will also take Bank Voles and small birds. Short-eared Owls nest on the ground in heather and grass but are a very rare breeding species in Ireland. In late autumn birds arrive along coastal areas and disperse to suitable wintering grounds. In some areas where prey is plentiful, small groups of Short-eared Owls can gather and hunt alongside each other. This bird was one of three that were hunting over grasslands near Ashbourne, Meath.

Red Squirrel

Sciurus vulgaris
Iora rua

The first sign of a Red Squirrel is often the pile of scales of pine cones and stripped cones that accumulate beneath a favoured feeding location. Sometimes when the squirrel is actively feeding there is a steady rain of scales audibly detectable as they fall through the branches. During the two mating seasons, in winter and early summer, a hectic commotion in the treetops may signify that a mating chase is in progress. These may be quite frantic and often involve more than one competing male in pursuit of a fertile female. In good years female squirrels may breed twice, but more usually they have one litter of usually three (one to six) kittens. Red Squirrels do not hibernate, although they may spend more time in their dreys (nests) when the weather is cold.

The Red Squirrel is our only native squirrel, although it almost became extinct during the 18th century owing to hunting for skins and deforestation. In the 19th century the remnants were supplemented by squirrels from England and by the early 20th century it was re-established in almost all counties. It is now in decline again because of the impact of the introduced Grey Squirrel. Red Squirrels cannot cope well with tannins and so must wait until acorns, which are not their principal natural food, are well-ripened before they can feed on them. This is not a problem for Grey Squirrels who can exploit the acorns earlier in the season. Grey Squirrels also carry a poxvirus which evolved with them in north America and to which they are largely immune as a consequence. Red Squirrels are vulnerable because they have only come into contact with Grey Squirrels within the past 100 years and have not yet evolved immunity to the virus.

The Red Squirrel is a small squirrel whose overall colour is brown, although it may range from greyish-brown on the one hand, to chestnut red on the other. In summer it is chestnut red with a paler, bushy tail. The winter coat is darker and so is the tail. The ears are rounded but they appear pointed because of the tuft of hair that grows along the margin. In summer these hairs are relatively short and pale but in the autumn moult they are replaced by longer, darker hairs and therefore appear triangular.

Red Squirrels are creatures of pine forests but will thrive in mixed and deciduous woodland and parkland when Grey Squirrels are not present. Their breeding and survival are very sensitive to food supply and they eat buds, shoots, flowers, bark, insects, berries, orchard fruits, seeds, nuts, fungi and lichens in season.

Waxwing

Bombycilla garrulus
Síodeiteach

Waxwings are Starling-sized birds, with long crests and colourful wings and tails. Red, waxy appendages on some wing feathers give the species their name. Breeding in northern Europe, they are extremely tame and very vocal, giving loud, trilling calls. In summer they catch insects but in winter survive by eating a variety of berries. It appears that the birds tend to prefer red berries to paler berries because, just like apples, the red are sweeter, having a higher sugar content. Waxwings will come to the ground to eat fallen berries and visit pools to drink. Occasionally Ireland experiences so-called irruptions of Waxwings. This happens when there are fewer berries than normal to sustain the birds in their traditional European wintering grounds and birds sweep westwards in search of food. In some years hundreds of birds can gather in large flocks. This bird was photographed in north Dublin in early 2009.

Blackbird

Blackbird

Turdus merula
Céirseach

In winter the population of thrushes increases with the arrival of birds from northern Europe. The weather there is simply too severe for many species to survive. Among these are familiar breeding species such as Blackbirds, Song and Mistle Thrushes as well as Redwings and Fieldfares, the latter often referred to as 'winter thrushes'. When really cold weather grips Europe, even larger numbers of thrushes arrive along the east coast as these birds, wintering on the continent or even in Britain, sweep westwards to Ireland, trying to take advantage of our milder winters. Many of these form large flocks and are found in habitats from gardens to open pastures. They will take a variety of food, from earthworms to fruit and, just like Waxwings, they will also eat berries when available. This male Blackbird was photographed in Dublin.

Mistle Thrush

Turdus viscivorus
Liatráisc

A common, resident breeding species, Mistle Thrushes are the largest member of the thrush family that occurs in Ireland. Both male and female appear identical. In winter European birds join our Irish birds and seek food in a variety of habitats. Resident birds, however, try to defend their territories in winter. They give loud, rattling alarm calls and aggressively see off other species that try to feed in their areas. Pairs will also defend favourite trees or bushes that supply them with berries throughout the winter. This bird was photographed in Dublin as it tried to defend its berry supply against a large flock of Waxwings that had just arrived into the area.

Fieldfare

Turdus pilaris
Sacán

Redwing

Turdus iliacus
Deargán sneachta

Known collectively as 'winter thrushes', Fieldfares and Redwings are purely winter visitors to Ireland and are found in large, roving flocks throughout the country. Fieldfares are the larger of the two and breed in northern Europe. Redwings breed both in northern Europe and Iceland. Like other thrush species, they struggle to find food in extreme weather conditions and will take worms, berries and fruit. These images were captured during the cold winter of December 2009/January 2010 when birds were fleeing the extreme weather of mainland Europe. Reaching Ireland, they found Ireland gripped by similar weather. It was estimated that many tens of thousands of Redwings and Fieldfares died of starvation and exhaustion during that period. This Fieldfare was visiting a garden in Dublin and was defending a supply of apples against all other birds. The Redwing was part of a large flock feeding on grasslands near Killarney, Kerry.

Twite

Carduelis flavirostris
Gleoiseach sléibhe

An uncommon, resident breeding species confined to northern and western regions, Twite have a wide global range extending from Ireland across north-west Europe and into the Himalayas. Males show a bright pink rump, and in summer show a dark bill. In winter the bill turns yellow. Females are similar but do not have the bright pink rump. Twites nest in old walls or in clumps of heather and gorse. However, due to habitat loss the population of Twite has declined in recent years. In addition to this, the departure from the farming of grain crops has impacted on the birds as the spillage from such grain harvesting provided Twite (and other bird species) with a valuable source of rich winter feeding. This male was photographed at Raghly Pier, Sligo.

Song Thrush

Turdus philomelos
Smólach ceoil

The smallest and shyest member of our breeding thrush species, the Song Thrush is a bird of woodlands, hedgerows and gardens. Preferring to forage for food among the leaf litter of woodlands or under hedges, our birds tend not to feed out in the open like Mistle Thrushes. However, like other thrush species, our population increases each winter with the arrival of birds from Europe, and these Song Thrushes can be found feeding alongside Redwings and Fieldfares on open pastures. In harsh winter weather all thrushes struggle to find worms and larvae on open pastures. This Song Thrush was photographed in Kerry.

Pygmy Shrew

Sorex minutus
Dallóg fhraoigh

The Pygmy Shrew has been here for at least 8,000 years. They are the smallest of Ireland's native mammals and, as result, have a number of interesting features. They are highly territorial and agressive towards one another and were it not for a brief lull in hostilities between males and females the species would not exist at all. They live short, hectic lives. Because they are so small, they need to feed within three hours of the previous meal and must consume at least their body weight in food each day. Because they lack the sophisticated physiology of bats they cannot hibernate, and so they are almost continuously active all year round. Even when resting, which is almost never, their little hearts pump at about 600 beats per minute and when active can beat as fast as 1,000 per minute. After about 15 months, and about 525 million heartbeats, they die of extreme old age. Most are born in June and July but breeding may occur between April and October. About three-quarters of Pygmy Shrews die before being old enough to breed and those that do usually die during the winter. The population is maintained by non-breeding juveniles who survive the winter to reproduce the following summer.

Pygmy Shrews are found in grassland, hedges, woodlands, peatlands — in fact almost anywhere with dense ground cover. Children, particularly, may be able to hear their high-pitched twittering and whistling in long grass during the summer months. Pygmy Shrews build spherical nests hidden in vegetation or under logs or rocks. Because of their prodigious appetites they are fiercely territorial and are opportunistic predators that eat almost anything they can overpower such as beetles (mostly), woodlice, flies, bugs, insect larvae and spiders. In their turn, although many predators find them distasteful, Pygmy Shrews are eaten by foxes and they may form up to a quarter of the diet of Barn Owls during the early part of the year.

Smooth Newt

Lissotriton vulgaris
Earc lúachra

When the Smooth Newt emerges from hibernation quite early in the year, in January or February, just like the frog, it has breeding on its mind. It has spent the winter in a frost-free recess in a wall, under logs or other secluded sites and now makes for the water. Smooth Newts breed in still or sluggish water such as drains, natural ponds or garden ponds, particularly if there is submerged vegetation on which to attach their eggs. The male at this time sports a splendid nuptial dress of a crest along his back, a bluish line along his flanks and tail and an orange throat and belly and webbed hind feet. The males are about the same size as females but their tail is longer. The tail is used as an element in a courtship ritual in an attempt to persuade a female to mate.

If a female has been suitably induced, the male then deposits his sperm in a convenient package on an underwater structure from which it is collected by the female. The female uses the sperm in the package to fertilise her 300 or so eggs which are laid one at a time and attached to the stem or leaf of an aquatic plant.

By April or so breeding is over, the males have resumed their more normal garb and the adults may leave the breeding pond more or less permanently and go their separate ways until the following spring. Meanwhile the tadpoles (efts) hatch and grow, feeding on aquatic animals. They are quite ferocious predators and will eat anything that their mouths can cope with. They begin with tiny zooplankton such as water fleas and graduate to larger prey as the grow. They are not averse to cannibalism. Efts can be distinguished from frog tadpoles by the fact that their front legs develop before their hind legs. It is the reverse with frogs. By late summer or early autumn the juveniles replace their feathery gills with internal lungs and leave the water. Outside of the breeding season the Smooth Newts move to damp habitats such as marshy patches, long grass, damp scrub and wet woodland. There they feed on terrestrial worms, slugs, insects and other invertebrates and also aquatic and semi-aquatic invertebrates. They will not return fully to water for up to three years by which time they themselves are mature enough to breed.

Blackcap

Sylvia atricapilla
Caipín dubh

A member of the warbler family, Blackcaps are a widespread breeding, summer migrant species from southern Europe. As our breeding birds move south towards the Mediterranean regions in autumn, they are replaced by birds from central Europe that come to spend the winter in Ireland. Males show the black crown from which the species derives its name; females have a chestnut-coloured crown. They are particularly fond of fruit, with apples being a favourite. In harsh winters Blackcaps depend on such fruit to survive. They will also eat berries and, where possible, will hunt insects. The male bird was photographed in Dublin while the female was visiting a garden in Louth.

House Mouse

Mus domesticus
Luch thí

The House Mouse began its existence as a creature of the grassy steppes of central Asia, sheltering in rock crevices and living on seeds of grasses and other plants. Once it developed an association with humans and their settlements, its global spread was more or less assured and it now has a worldwide distribution. It is probably the most familiar mammalian pest of all and there can be few people who have not seen a House Mouse.

Because of its association with humans it has access to a reliable supply of food and shelter. As a result it has become omnivorous and its diet is greatly variable and depends very much on what is available. It is now more or less confined to a life indoors in dwellings, warehouses or farm buildings and shows little tendency to live outdoors. It occasionally ventures into hedgerows during the summer but generally dislikes open spaces. House Mice have quite a variable social structure depending on local circumstances. Their breeding has also been disconnected from the seasons and House Mice will breed all the year round when conditions are suitable. Female House Mice can breed early and often, beginning at about eight weeks of age and often achieving ten litters a year. It is not surprising that a population may increase six- to eight-fold in a single year. Associated with this impressive reproductive rate is their tolerance of crowding and, as a result, population densities may be quite high. It is probably therefore fortunate for householders that House Mice are nocturnal.

House Mice, despite their restricted distribution, are an important prey species for Barn Owls, Kestrels, foxes, stoats and cats. They are quite sensitive to cold, and hard winters play a key role in controlling numbers, particularly in unheated buildings. House Mice in their biology and lifestyle have much to interest the biologist but most people would prefer not to have the opportunity to study House Mice at large in their own homes.

Stonechat

Saxicola torquatus
Caislín cloch

A common, resident breeding species found in a wide variety of habitats, from upland bogs and mountain valleys to young forestry plantations, rough pastures and coastal dune systems. Birds nest under cover in areas of thick hedgerows and gorse. In winter, birds migrate to low-lying and coastal areas where food is more plentiful. During extremely cold winters, Stonechats struggle to find enough food and large numbers can die if such extreme conditions persist for long periods. This male was one of over 40 Stonechats that had gathered around large mounds of rotting seaweed at Blackrock Strand, Kerry, during severely cold weather. Like other species, the birds were taking advantage of the large numbers of insects that can be found in the seaweed.

Bearded Reedling

Panurus biarmicus
Meantán croiméalach

Bearded Reedlings are found in large areas of reedbed. They feed on insects during the summer and on seeds in winter. During the late 1970s and early 1980s Ireland had a very small breeding population, at just two localities in Cork and Wicklow. It was thought likely that these birds may have become extinct as a result of several very cold winters. In 1990 a single female was seen in Wexford but the species was not recorded again in Ireland for over 20 years until, in the winter of 2010, seven birds were found in Wexford. They were present in a large reedbed and, in the summer of 2011, raised at least one family, successfully establishing Bearded Reedling back as an Irish breeding species. The brightly coloured male shows the long, black feathers on the face from which the species derives its name. The duller female lacks such distinctive feathers. These birds were photographed in Wexford. They frequently came out of the reeds to drink rainwater that had gathered in a small pool in a shallow hollow of a nearby rock.

Winter Garden Finches

In late autumn and early winter Ireland sees the arrival of large numbers of finches from Europe. These birds move out of Europe to avoid harsh winter weather conditions and add to the population of our resident finches. They can form large, mixed flocks and move together in search of food. Garden feeding stations provide a plentiful supply of food and attract a wide range of species including Siskins, Redpolls and Goldfinches which are able to feed from hanging seed and nut feeders. Below them birds such as Chaffinches gather any fallen seeds on the ground. Goldfinches are a relatively recent addition to such feeders and have now become a very common visitor to gardens in towns and cities. In some winters we are graced by the presence of Bramblings, a species that breeds in northern Europe. These birds never occur in summer. When they are found here, they are usually within flocks of Chaffinches. The Brambling, Chaffinch and Goldfinch pictured here were all part of a finch flock that was visiting a garden in Wicklow. The Redpoll was also photographed in Wicklow while the colourful male Siskin was photographed in Kerry.

Brambling
Fringilla montifringilla
Breacán

Goldfinch
Carduelis carduelis
Lasair choille

Chaffinch
Fringilla coelebs
Rí rua

Redpoll
Carduelis flammea
Deargéadan

Siskin
Carduelis spinus
Siscín

Long-tailed Tit

Aegithalos caudatus
Meantán earrfhada

A common, resident bird of woodlands, Long-tailed Tits move in small family parties through the canopy in search of insects and larvae. In summer they can be hard to see but give their presence away by their short, sharp contact calls as the birds keep in touch with each other. In winter, however, when the leaves are off the trees, these handsome, tiny birds are more easily seen and will join with other species of tits in large, roving flocks. They are extremely agile and will hang upside-down in search of food. In recent years they have discovered nut feeders and are now regular winter visitors to many gardens. This bird was photographed in the Botanic Gardens, Dublin.